scandimodern

scandimodern

Fay Sweet

MITCHELL BEAZLEY

← A summer house in the Gulf of Finland, owned and designed by architect Bertel Gripenberg, 1980.

Page 1 The Johnsen summer House in Risør, Norway, by architect Carl-Viggo Hølmebakk, 1997.

Pages 2–3 The Gunnlogson House in Rungsted, Denmark, by architect Halldor Gunnolgson, 1958.

scandimodern
Fay Sweet

First published in 2003 by Mitchell Beazley,
an imprint of Octopus Publishing Group Ltd, 2–4 Heron Quays, London E14 4JP

The publishers will be grateful for any information that will assist them in keeping future editions up to date. While every care has been taken in the preparation of this book, neither the author nor the publisher can accept any liability for any consequence arising from the use thereof, or the information contained therein.

ISBN 1 84000 735 4

A CIP record of this book is available from the British Library

Executive Art Editor Auberon Hedgecoe
Senior Editor Emily Anderson
Editor Lara Maiklem
Designer Geoff Borin
Picture Researcher Helen Stallion
Production Controller Gary Hayes
Proofreader Claire Musters
Indexer Helen Snaith

Set in Frutiger, Helvetica, and EuropeanPi

Printed and bound in China by Toppan Printing Company Limited

To order this book as a gift or an incentive contact Mitchell Beazley on 020 7531 8481

| contents | introduction 6 |

introduction

Sleek, open-plan spaces, large windows, natural timber, colourful rugs and blankets, blonde wood furniture, roaring fires and cast-iron stoves, elegant glassware ... ask anyone to describe the modern Scandinavian home and their replies are often the same. The style that evolved during the 20th century is instantly recognizable: a comfortable and welcoming place, filled with sensual shapes, materials, and textures, flooded with sunlight and fresh air in the summer and warm and cosy in the winter.

With its roots in the Modernism of Le Corbusier, Mies van der Rohe, and the Bauhaus, the Scandinavian style of Sweden, Finland, Denmark, and Norway grew away from the mainstream and evolved in its own distinctive way. Scandinavian designers gave a warm and human touch to the stripped-back simplicity and machine-made efficiency of Modernism. Designs have a clear practicality and honesty, chairs are simple and comfortable, lamps produce soft, diffused light, and scissors fit well in the hand. This soft Modernism appeals to our desire for a tranquil and well-ordered home, a space that is ergonomically and ecologically sound, and a refuge from the stresses of the outside world.

Just like the climate and the landscapes, Scandinavian architecture and design is characterized by exciting tensions and contrasts. An example of this is the tension between light and heat.

Although large windows let in sunlight, they also let in the cold, so designs have evolved that incorporate smart glass (a material with transparent coatings to control heat and cold entering and leaving through the glass), insulation, and careful orientation of the building to protect it from the worst weather. There is also the contrast that is made between inside and outside – the blurring of boundaries to draw nature inside, even in winter, while making outside "rooms" on sheltered decks and terraces to make the most of the sunlight. Scandinavian homes are fit for, and sympathetic to, their environment. For a century debate has raged on the relative merits of handmade and factory-made goods. The Scandinavian obsession is for affordable, elegant, well-designed products, but to achieve this, mass-production is essential. The challenge is in keeping the items user-friendly, beautiful, and well-made.

The roll call of world-class Scandinavian architects and designers is also a remarkable one: starting with such masters as Arne Jacobsen and Alvar Aalto, followed by Verner Panton, Jørn Utzon, and Nanna Ditzel, right up to the present day with Thomas Sandell, Stefan Lindfors, and Lena Bergström. Manufacturing names are equally impressive for their innovation, style, and consistent high quality – from Saab and Volvo to Bang & Olufsen, Nokia, Lego, Electrolux, Marimekko, Fiskars, and, of course, Ikea.

← Danish architect Jørn Utzon's Middlebøe House of 1953 at Lake Furesö, near Copenhagen. The rectangular box is raised above the water for better views. Access to the site was difficult so Utzon took the unusual step of using a pre-fabricated concrete frame, which was pieced together on site. The use of red and black reflects the architect's interest in Chinese architecture.

↑ The Siesby House, designed in 1957 by Arne Jacobsen, is set on a slope overlooking the Lyngby Lake in Denmark. The wooden rectangular box sits on a brick-built lower floor, the open-plan living space and huge floor-to-ceiling windows making the most of the views. The exterior walls are finished with vertical wood boards.

→ Villa Snellman, on the outskirts of Stockholm, was the first major work by the Swedish architect Erik Gunnar Asplund, in 1917. Asplund was among the pioneering designers to give a modern twist to Swedish Neo-classical design. This hall is oval-shaped and lined with wood.

↓ Entitled *Mother's and Little Girls' Room*, this 1897 watercolour by Swedish artist Carl Larsson caused a furore when it was exhibited, by depicting informal, bohemian family life at a time when semi-naked children and the chaos of everyday living were not considered suitable subjects for a work of art.

→ The Stucco Craftsman's House in Stockholm was the home of Axel Notini, who used his skills in the 1880s and '90s to lavishly decorate the interior – it became a showpiece for his craft. In the following decades this dark, richly embellished style of interior was to be replaced with an altogether simpler and lighter finish.

dawn of the new world

At the turn of the 20th century, the Scandinavian home was very much like any other in the industrialized world. Impoverished people, particularly those in the towns and cities, lived in squalid and cramped conditions. Those in the countryside lived simple and often hard lives in basic homes with few amenities. Poverty was rife, comfort was rare. The middle classes, meanwhile, dressed their homes with heavily decorated, dark wood furniture, windows were shrouded in thick curtains, and every surface was muffled with rugs and drapes. The gloomy, stifling interiors were pieced together as an ostentatious display of affluence and accepted good taste.

Then came a wave of radical change, the product of a collision of events and factors. First, the Industrial Revolution arrived. Alongside this came a rediscovery of national identity; social reformers and designers shared a vision of how the world could be a better place for all. With industrialization came a migration of people to the big cities in search of work. Stockholm, Helsinki, Oslo, and Copenhagen each saw their populations escalate, but this growth could not be matched by the pace of building new homes, which remained slow. In the late 1800s there was already serious concern about conditions and welfare, and ideas began to be formulated in order to improve the situation. In common with the Arts and Crafts movement in Britain, the Scandinavian reformers believed that design could be a force for good and an instrument of change. Numerous liberal-thinking architects were therefore motivated to start thinking and planning for a new and improved world. They became interested in making homes free of the old-fashioned trappings of wealth, in making them simpler, more hygienic, and more in tune with the natural environment.

The pretty, rural home of the Swedish artist Carl Larsson and his designer wife Karin provided to be the model that many would follow. The old farmhouse at Sundborn, just north of Stockholm, was simply decorated and furnished with painted furniture. This Swedish rustic style was far from being ostentatious or impressive, instead it created an informal, family home. The sun-filled interiors and happy, playful children were painted by Carl and published in 1899 in a book of watercolours. He felt that it was not only his job as an artist to preach the joy of beauty, but also his social duty to show the masses how to create a functional, charming, and inexpensive interior. The book – *Ett hem* (A Home) – was sold in tens of thousands throughout Scandinavia and northern Europe, and inspired change in millions of homes.

the arrival of modernism

While the Scandinavian countries were becoming accustomed to industrialization and the expansion of their cities, they were also undergoing massive national change. In 1905 Norway won its freedom from the union with Sweden (it had been ruled by Denmark from 1536 to 1814, and still retained a Danish King until 1905), and Finland gained independence from Russia in 1917. Meanwhile, Denmark was growing used to life with a much-reduced empire and new social democratic politics.

In each case these northern countries had to reinvent themselves, and each chose to do so by looking back and reflecting on its own cultural heritage, particularly traditional architecture and design. However, they were also looking for a fresh start, which meant that they needed to create a dynamic, forward-looking image in order to cultivate a thriving economy. No one was going to buy goods from some forgotten northern backwater, and Modernist design provided the route they needed in order to be taken seriously. The most successful designers of the time, such as Alvar Aalto in Finland, demonstrated their brilliance by taking the new so-called International Style and making it their own. Aalto fused Modernism with the essence of Finnishness by celebrating local materials, such as birch, and tapping into local craft skills. This not only won him admiration at home, but also secured him, and Finland, a position on the world stage.

While seeking a new national style for their designs, these early Scandinavian Modernist pioneers not only took their inspiration from their immediate surroundings but also from further afield. The national architecture magazines of the day published projects from all around the world, and curious young architects made trips throughout Europe to further their education and see for themselves what was happening in the exciting world of Modern architecture. The young Aalto was no exception, and he made numerous trips abroad; one such trip to Italy in the 1920s had a lasting effect on his designs.

Aalto's Danish contemporary, Arne Jacobsen, also visited Italy in the 1920s. Although the influence of Japanese design is unmistakable in many of his projects, the clean-edged, white Modernist buildings he saw in Europe were what really captured his imagination at the start of his career. However, by the 1940s and '50s the edges had softened, and Jacobsen made greater use of brick and timber, and created his famous organic-shaped furniture, such as the Egg, Swan, and Ant chairs.

← This simple summer house at Tisvilde, Denmark was designed in 1956 by Arne Jacobsen. Raised up, it has one continuous glass wall to enjoy the waterside views. The wooden frame is clad with pine treated with preservative on the outside, and untreated pine on the inside. The chimney rises from the wood-burning stove – a focal point of the living room.

↑ The Riihitie House in Helsinki was designed
between 1935 and 1936 by Alvar Aalto as
his own house and studio. The studio, in the
background, could be separated from the
living space by a large sliding plywood panel.
The room has a huge double-glazed window
overlooking the garden, and includes a built-in
window seat and flower boxes.

← In the simple but elegant home of Swedish glass and textile designer Lena Bergström, the shaped ply dining chairs by Danish designer Arne Jacobsen look as good today as when they were designed in the 1950s. The glass pendant lamps, vase, and pebble-shaped candle holders were all designed by Bergström.

→ This vibrant, oversized pop-art flower print is a classic from Finnish textile house Marimekko. The design, called Unikko (Poppy), by Maija Isola is an all-time classic for the company, which was founded in the 1950s. In the early 21st century the company is once again enjoying a renaissance of interest in its classic, simple clothing, and colourful textiles.

a new confidence

The post-war years have seen intense experimentation and cultural expansion in Scandinavian countries. At the forefront, design ideas have included radically rethinking interior spaces – open-plan living that suits modern, informal lifestyles, and sliding walls and doors that make spaces more flexible. Experimentation with materials has introduced the idea of homes made, for example, from prefabricated panels. Traditional materials – wood, brick, and occasionally stone – have been mixed with new ones, such as steel and concrete. In general, in all the Scandinavian countries the plentiful supply of timber and close affinity with nature has been coupled with a growing interest in ecological building and design. Furniture and furnishings, meanwhile, have been revolutionized by innovative manufacturing techniques, particularly for plywood. Flat sheets can now be curved and moulded to make appealing ergonomic furniture.

The surge of interest in Scandinavian design reached a peak in the 1950s and '60s, when it was being exhibited worldwide and published in virtually every home-style magazine. However, it was a high that was impossible to sustain. During the 1970s the focus of attention was switched to early ergonomic and ecological

design. Then, in the 1980s, the Scandinavian Modern look merged with a tidal wave of new, sleek interiors, furniture, and accessories; products from Italy, France, the United States, and Britain became virtually indistinguishable from those of the Scandinavian countries.

However, at the turn of this new century there are clear signs of a Scandinavian renaissance. Writers such as Ibsen, painters such as Munch, composers such as Jean Sibelius and Carl Nielsen, and architects Arne Jacobsen, Erik Gunnar Asplund, Alvar Aalto, and Jørn Utzon are continually being reappraised, and are growing in stature. More recently, Swedish band Koop and Norwegians Röyksopp are attracting huge followings for their dance music. Finnish composers Kaija Saariaho and Magnus Lindberg fill concert halls worldwide, and artists Olav Christopher Jenssen and Stefan Lindfors draw international acclaim. Designers including Thomas Sandell and Lena Bergström are becoming household names and producing exquisite work, which, once again, finds its roots in the culture, design heritage, and landscape of their native countries. In addition, the big manufacturers such as Artek, Ikea, Orrefors, Nokia, Bang & Olufsen, and Marimekko have become inspirational leaders in their respective fields, and are selling their highly desirable wares in growing numbers of stores around the world.

rural

roots in nature

In telling the story of Scandinavian Modern design, it is impossible to overstate the importance of rural culture, along with its architectural and design heritage. The countryside can be credited as a key inspiration for the distinctive new look and design.

When a changing approach to architecture began to appear late in the 19th century, there was the brief emergence of a style that has come to be known as National Romanticism. It was a nostalgic reworking of traditional architecture, much of it rural. Often the results were heavy, safe, and solid, and featured ornate stone and wood decoration.

The concern for preserving rural crafts and traditional skills was felt keenly. In Sweden, for example, in the late 1800s people feared for their fragile cultural heritage. They saw that the arrival of industrialization could mean the departure of tradition, and this provoked the founding of dozens of associations and societies to collect examples of ancient folk crafts. Every effort was made to preserve ancient skills and encourage more people to learn them.

By the start of the 20th century, as Norway, Sweden, Finland, and Denmark were each redefining their respective national identities, they again looked to the countryside for inspiration. This was felt particularly strongly in Finland, where people looked eagerly for shards of the old culture that had survived despite centuries of occupation by Sweden and then Russia. Finnish master Alvar Aalto often described his admiration for buildings, such as the ancient peasant farmhouse, or tupa. This strong, timber-built home, with its single, multi-functional room and simple but practical furnishings, had an honesty and integrity that had a powerful appeal to the Modernist. He borrowed heavily from the tupa, reinventing it as simpler and more refined, retaining the open-plan living spaces and natural wood furniture.

Elsewhere, young architects and designers took study trips to old farmsteads and the great country houses, in order to rediscover their rich design heritage. For example, traditional Norwegian and Danish farmsteads that were built around courtyards inspired many modern architects to incorporate an enclosed yard idea in their designs. Among these was the Dane Jørn Utzon, who used the courtyard idea in countless projects. In Sweden, the "little red stuga", the traditional red-painted wooden farmhouse with white outlines around its windows and door, provided an ideal model for new rural homes. By rediscovering this heritage, understanding the building methods, and reminding themselves of who they were, the countries found a solid bedrock to act as foundations on which they could build for the future.

← Traditional Finnish tupas, or farmhouses, provided inspiration for countless modern architects, including Alvar Aalto. They have all the ingredients for simple living – a big open-plan living space, unpretentious wooden furniture, and hand-crafted striped rugs.

→ For Swedes, the little red stuga has an almost mythical status as the ideal home and rural retreat. The authentic version features a small porch and smoke curling from the chimney, it must be painted red, and edged in white. This drawing by Torben Grut dates from 1905, and is part of a plan for a do-it-yourself stuga.

← The living room at the Larsson family house in Sundborn, north of Stockholm. It marks a transitional moment in Swedish design at the end of the 19th century, when the dark and oppressive interiors were left behind in favour of light, open spaces.

creators of the swedish style

The rebirth of new Scandinavian countries at the turn of the 20th century was not a single-track route. Along with the industrialists and politicians, who were interested in creating powerful and thriving modern industrialized nations, were groups of intellectuals, social reformers, architects, and artists. While some of them focused on the health of the nation's culture, including the threat to traditional skills posed by the machine, others wanted to improve living conditions for the poor, and many were interested in new ways of living by casting off the vulgar, ostentatious, and formal Victorian and Teutonic interior and architectural design styles of the 19th century.

In Sweden, the artist Carl Larsson and his designer wife Karin created Sundborn, a countryside home so refreshingly simple and beautiful, and so inspiring, that they alone have been hailed as the "creators of the Swedish Style". Sundborn came to the nation's attention when Carl Larsson's 24 watercolour paintings of the interiors were published in 1899 in the book *Ett hem* (A Home). Larsson was already famous and much admired for his work, which included the huge murals at the National Museum, Opera House, and National Theatre in Stockholm, and the book was eagerly received. However, reactions were divided. Some were shocked by the sparsely furnished rooms, strewn with the debris of everyday life, while many warmed to the sunny, informal bohemian lifestyle.

The most appealing and distinguishing characteristics of the Sundborn home were the light and airy interiors, old and new colourful painted furniture, chequered and striped fabrics, muslin drapes, embroidered and woven rugs, cushions and throws, and painted wall decorations. The book enabled the simple, rural look to be adopted in millions of Swedish rural and urban homes, and for it to be adapted to suit the tastes of other Scandinavian and north European homes in the following century.

While the Larssons were making this Utopia in Sundborn, they were not alone in their dreams. Throughout Europe, artists and architects were developing the idea of the artistic house. The seeds of this idea were sown by British designer and socialist William Morris, a key figure in the Arts and Crafts Movement. He linked a number of concerns – that the machine would destroy the natural expression of creativity and craft, that beauty in art and design could enrich lives, and that improved living conditions should be a priority for the poor. These ideas were discussed at length in the British magazine *The Studio*, to which the Larssons subscribed.

→ Carl Larsson's bedroom at the Sundborn house. The simplicity of this built-in and white-painted bed with its plain curtains would have astonished the Swedish middle-classes who, at the time, were used to decorating their homes with more ostentatious furniture and textiles, as a show of wealth and good taste.

In 1888 the Larssons were given, as a present from Karin's father, the house called Lilla Hyttnäs. This house became enormously influential, and eventually engendered a design revolution. The property was a simple, two-storey rural cottage, built in a glorious setting close to Lake Siljan and the Sundborn river. Carl Larsson seemed unimpressed with his first sight of the place – "It was a very small, unpretentious, rather ugly, insignificant building, built on a waste slag, appropriately named Hyttnas". (Hyttnas translates as a smelting house on a spit of land). However, once inside Larsson was smitten. "Here I experienced that unspeakably sweet feeling of seclusion from the clamour and noise of the world." At first the house was used as a summer retreat, but, as the Larssons extended, remodelled, and decorated, it eventually became their permanent home, and a work of art in progress. Carl contributed murals, stained glass, and portraits of the children and family life, and Karin created embroideries and tapestries, and designed furniture.

The success of the Larssons' home was that it idealized rural life, previously dismissed by the middle-classes as unsophisticated, primitive, and poverty-stricken. The Larssons' reinterpretation was as a healthy, pleasurable, simple, inexpensive, and informal way of living that celebrated folk art and incorporated the familiar, robust, and comfortable furniture and furnishings of a farmhouse. However, this did not impress every visitor. In one document Carl Larsson recalls reactions to his bedroom – "People say it is so healthy to have one's bedstead in the middle of the floor, but I did not know that when we decided to put it there. A neighbour of mine – I wonder if it was the major – is supposed to have said it looks like a man-servant's room. Men who come of ancient stock consider it right to lie on feather beds between linen sheets and with pillows trimmed with lace, coquettish and neat in every way. But in my simple bed, on my straw mattress, I sleep well and deeply, like a king lying 'in state'. Now and again I paint the walls of the room with chalk and distemper; it then becomes as clean and bright as some heavenly dwelling."

This apparently effortless style captured the imaginations of many, including important social reformers such as Ellen Key, who was moved by seeing Larsson's watercolours at the Stockholm exhibition of art and industry in 1897. Key joined with Larsson in believing that the power of art could improve health and wellbeing. In 1899 she expressed these ideas in her own hugely popular and influential publication *Skönhet för Alla* (Beauty for Everyone).

← This decorative doorway between bedrooms is the work of Karin Larsson. The frame is painted with a lily, carnations, and bluebells, and the unusual, open-weave hanging curtain features a stylized "Rose of Love". The curtains provide privacy without completely blocking out the light flow between the rooms.

→ The dining room has a striking red and green colour scheme – green is used on the wooden wall panelling, and red is used on the chairs, the in-built window seat, window frame, and shelves. This is the warm heart of the home, as featured in Larsson's famous book of watercolours *Ett hem* (A Home).

→ Villa Mairea at Noormarkku was designed by architect Alvar Aalto, 1938–41. At the time this was an ultra-modern villa, with its teak-clad living room that projects out into the garden and forms a sunny terrace area for the master bedroom above.

↓ The interior of Villa Mairea echoes the surrounding forest with an exciting screen of irregularly spaced columns that stand like a small copse of trees around the open stair. The larger, black-painted steel columns are wrapped with rattan and birch strips, a decorative feature and also a reminder that nature can be found both inside and out.

→ The big fireplace sitting in the corner of the living area is a soft-shaped feature. Nicknamed "Aalto's ear" in the architect's office, it resembles the shape that might be formed by the wind in a snowdrift.

bringing nature inside – alvar aalto

There are few homes that so thoroughly and cleverly synthesize rural landscape with modern architecture as the Villa Mairea, designed in the late 1930s by Finnish architect Alvar Aalto. It is a treasury of design detail, luscious materials, and references to the surrounding pine forest. From a distance the outline of the two-storey, white box villa is evident but, close-up, there can be no doubt that the landscape is drawn into the house as much as the house is drawn into the landscape.

The entrance is protected by a large, sheltering canopy, its curved, meandering shape echoing the coastline of a lake, or an awning of tree branches. The canopy is held aloft by a "forest" of spindly sapling columns. Inside, a further "copse" of columns, irregularly spaced, filters light through the main living room and wraps around the open-tread stair. In the open-plan living area some columns are wrapped in rattan to evoke the bark of trees. Even the subtly changing floor levels give the house a settled feel, accommodating the contours of the land below. The change in floor levels also adds visual interest to the space, and helps to divide it into different areas: a place for sitting around the fire with friends, a place for reading, a place for working, and so on.

Villa Mairea is set in a large estate at Noormarkku, a few miles inland on the west coast of Finland. It was built for Harry and Maire Gullichsen for use as a summer house, and was intended as an expression of the client's view of modern life. Aalto's first proposal, a rustic hut modelled on traditional farmhouses, was abandoned in favour of his upgraded designs, partially inspired by Frank Lloyd Wright's Fallingwater in Pennsylvania, USA. With his new design Aalto could push his ideas further to include first-floor balconies, open living-spaces, and a rich palette of materials. Even the stone detailing outside is reminiscent of Fallingwater, where slabs are laid in horizontal bands to resemble the natural strata of rock.

The collage of materials is impressive, both inside and out. Outside, the first-floor studio is wrapped with weatherboarding, while the ground-floor living area is cased in rich teak and dark stone. Inside, ceilings are finished in panels of slender wood strips, and floors work their way from red slate at the entrance to ceramic tiles, pale beech, and stone around the fireplaces. The wonderful detailing reaches a crescendo in the fireplace, where the white-plaster chimney breast is given an intriguing sculptural nook, not unlike a drift of wind-sculpted snow, that was nicknamed by fellow designers in the architect's studio as "Aalto's ear".

laboratories of ideas

Throughout the 20th century, while most new homes were being built in the rapidly expanding towns and cities, the modern rural house provided architects and designers with the opportunity to experiment. In an era when many architects felt driven to build better homes for the masses, creating one-off places for the affluent was justified as providing laboratories for design ideas, which could then be applied to urban housing. Such transferable ideas have included, among others, ways of coping with extremes of weather, bringing in more light with large, double- and triple-glazed windows, the economic use of materials made possible by a better understanding of structural engineering, unusual and ergonomically informed interior layouts, and energy efficiency.

One such laboratory of ideas was the Markelius House, in Kevinge, Sweden, built in 1945 by architect Sven Markelius for his family. A long, single-storey building, with an annex placed at right angles to the main house, it has tall brick chimneys, is clad in wood, and features a horizontal band of large and small windows. Although it has a reassuringly traditional feel, it is, in fact, constructed with prefabricated panels and designed with a flexible, modern interior space. In the aftermath of World War II this provided a powerful image of the good life, and presented a new way of informal living, now known as "Scandinavian Modern".

While early 20th-century Scandinavian architects were intent on making homes that were modern as well as expressions of national style, they were far from being closed to outside influences. Many architects, Alvar Aalto and Arne Jacobsen among them, had travelled extensively throughout Europe and the USA. Arne Jacobsen moved from Denmark to Sweden during World War II and then, in 1949, won a travel scholarship to Mexico and the USA, where he spent a week with Frank Lloyd Wright in his Taliesin East studio, and met Mies van der Rohe in Chicago. Scandinavian architects also kept in touch through architecture magazines and books. Japanese design, in particular, captured many imaginations – not least because of the distinct similarities between Scandinavia and Japan in terms of an affinity with nature, a romanticized view of the rural way of life, and a long tradition of using natural materials in skilful and beautiful ways.

This cross-pollination of ideas produced homes of great vibrancy. Influences from the USA and Japan were regularly fused with Scandinavian style. Jørn Utzon, in designing his own house at Hellebæk, in Northern Zealand, Denmark in 1952, acknowledges

← This house in the woods, Villa Schreiner, is by much-respected Norwegian architect Sverre Fehn. The well-weathered exterior and extensive use of glass make the house almost disappear among the trees.

→ Nature is welcomed inside this home with an interior wrapped in horizontal pine-boarding, along with the solid wood table and dining chairs. Textural contrast is provided in the monumental brick fireplace with in-built bench seat. While one side of the room is open to the garden, soft light is also filtered through the high-level, horizontal windows.

↑ The Johnsen Summer House at Risør, by Norwegian architect Carl-Viggo Hølmebakk, 1997. The clients had owned the site for 25 years and loved the outcrop of seven trees, which are now incorporated into the house.

the triple influences of Mies van der Rohe, Frank Lloyd Wright, and Japanese style. The house is a long, single-storey box, in Danish yellow brick, encorporating an entire glass wall that overlooks the valley beyond. Outside is a series of elegant, stepped, brick terraces – the effect is one of restrained elegance. These influences appear again in the very different Middlebøe House, which Utzon designed overlooking Lake Furesö, near Copenhagen, in 1953. The Farnsworth House in the USA, completed by Mies van der Rohe just a couple of years earlier, is clearly a major influence, but instead of using a steel frame Utzon designed an innovative concrete frame system. Both of these Utzon houses were copied extensively.

Japanese influence is at its most powerful in projects such as the highly innovative guest annexe designed in 1957 by Vilhelm Wohlert for Nobel Prize-winning nuclear physicist Nils Bohr. This Danish project once again takes the single-storey box as its basis, but here the excitement is in the way it functions. In winter it is a mysterious, closed, black box; then, in summer, it bursts open and the shutters swing upwards to make sun shades for the guest bedrooms and long timber terrace.

The Japanese love of natural materials is echoed in architect Halldor Gunnløgsson's 1958 house at Rungsted, Strandvej, near Copenhagen. Black-stained and black-lacquered timber is used for the walls and doors, and is placed alongside screens of bamboo, natural timber ceilings, huge sliding glass windows, and a pristine, grey stone floor. The visionary, all-white, fitted kitchen with stainless-steel worktops still looks fantastic and modern after more than four decades of use.

Even now experimentation with rural housing continues to deliver exciting results. One of the most astonishing-looking projects in recent years is Norwegian architect Carl-Viggo Hølmebakk's Johnsen Summer House in Risør, Norway. This timber house, complete with wrap-around deck and featuring exquisite joinery, was completed in the late 1990s. The land itself had been owned by the clients for a quarter of a century, so they had plenty of time to explore and appreciate its natural qualities. They particularly liked one outcrop of rock and its collection of seven pine trees so, to celebrate the place, the house was designed to fit around and inside the stand of trees. Among the challenges facing Hølmebakk was how to build without harming the environment, particularly the tree roots. A computerized survey was made of the site, and a type of floating design was created that uses posts sunk into the ground, thus avoiding the tree roots. Inside the house, the rooms wrap round the trees, and the ceiling- and floor-levels differ to fit between the branches.

rural idyll

A warm and inviting home is an absolute must for all Scandinavians, especially those who have chosen to set up home, or enjoy taking their holidays, in the countryside. All the Scandinavian countries experience extremes in climate and can be plunged into freezing temperatures for months at a time. In such an environment a sense of coziness is essential, in fact the Danish even have a word for it, *hygge*, which, although difficult to translate directly, is generally taken to suggest the soft, warm, reassuring glow of being in a comfortable, feel-good place, surrounded by family and friends.

Over the last 50 years Scandinavian homes have become synonymous with warmth, comfort, tranquillity, and orderliness. They are usually built from natural materials using pioneering ecological building techniques and products. Their standards of energy efficiency are the envy of the rest of the world and have become the benchmark of

↓ In this house, the warm glow of pine mixed with rich, exposed brickwork combines to make an inviting interior. This home, designed in the late 1960s by the internationally renowned Norwegian architect Sverre Fehn, has a tranquil and timeless quality.

quality for house-builders everywhere. Although each country has evolved its own particular building style, they do have shared goals and aspirations, which include energy efficiency, sustainability, sensitivity to location, and the creation of highly desirable and particularly flexible, open-plan interiors.

Wood is the main house-building material used in most of Scandinavia – particularly in Norway, Sweden, and Finland – although nowadays it is often combined with concrete, steel, and stone. Brick is used prolifically in Danish house building but is only used in Norway and Sweden when the owner has specifically requested it and is prepared to pay the hugely increased cost of using the material. This premium can be as much as three times the price of building in wood. The Norwegian home shown above and left was designed in 1967 by the internationally famous architect Sverre Fehn. Here, brick is used as a luxurious addition to the interior and has been left in its natural state to add an intense richness to the colour palette. The owners of this house specifically asked for a home that

↑ Together with all the fitted cupboards and furniture, architect Sverre Fehn also designed the kitchen, which still has a modern feel to it decades later. Views of the forested landscape are maximized everywhere – there is even a long horizontal window slot between the worksurface and the wall-mounted cupboards.

↑ While this Danish kitchen and dining room has all the classic Scandinavian hallmarks – pale colours, natural woods, and a large open fireplace – there are also some Italian influences. The owners, who spent some time living in Italy, have introduced a generous white marble worksurface at the far end of the kitchen.

was cozy and intimate, so bare brick was used to add the extra warmth. However, the practicalities of using brick did prove to be a problem. Builders working in freezing winter temperatures had to work under a canopy of plastic in order to keep off the rain that threatened to freeze in the joints and blow the bricks apart. It is for reasons such as this that the brick manufacturing industry in Norway today has shrunk to just a handful of manufacturers, as bricks are only really used in larger buildings – for example, office blocks, hospitals, and schools.

In stark contrast to the problems encountered with brick, wood performs very well in extreme climates. It is an incredibly strong structural material, flexible and easy to use, a great natural insulator, and, of course, in Scandinavian countries it is in plentiful supply. Contrary to popular belief it also holds up well in the event of fire, as timber beams rarely burn right through; instead they char on the outside and retain their core strength for many hours. With its range of colours, intriguing textures, and patterns wood is also aesthetically appealing, and provides that much sought-after link with nature that, particularly these days, many people are seeking. Most importantly there are huge ecological benefits to using wood, as it is a natural and sustainable material.

The image of the modern Scandinavian rural home is an idyllic one: it usually enjoys a dramatic setting and is often surrounded by forests or open landscapes. To people from crowded, smaller countries, the sense of space and freedom is something that can only be be dreamed of. Perhaps their most appealing characteristic is their modern styling, which is perfectly suited to contemporary lives as they are light, open, and spacious, and often situated within easy reach of main towns and cities. With all this in mind it is easy to see that Scandinavians certainly know how to make the most of their landscape and homes.

↓ The small dining area within this kitchen was created by knocking down a wall and incorporating a smaller room – the bench seat disguises pipes that were difficult to move. The family wanted a relaxed feel and have blended traditional and modern styles, including the famous Arne Jacobsen-designed Series 7 chairs, seen here upholstered in luxurious black leather.

a converted barn – gotland, sweden

There is a strong Scandinavian affection for rural buildings; the simple building techniques, honest local materials, and generous spaces make them appealing homes. The converted barn shown here is located on the Swedish island of Gotland, and is a very good example of how these traditional characteristics have been retained. The barn is part of a farm complex, and the owners specifically wanted to keep a sense of the old vernacular architecture while, at the same time, also making a comfortable family summer house. True to so many rural Scandinavian retreats, it is situated in a beautiful woodland setting.

Despite its age the barn was in good condition, so during the restoration the owners managed to retain as much of the old structure as they could – this included some stone walls that they have exposed. Unfortunately, they were unable to save the traditional timber shingles on the roof and have replaced them with simple metal sheeting. The large internal spaces have been kept, with the living area opening a full nine metres (29½ft) up into the rafters. The family use the house to entertain friends, and enjoy long, summer suppers around the huge refectory table. Above the kitchen, with its large, restaurant-style zinc worktops, is the open sleeping area where parents' and children's beds are separated by large hanging textiles. Opposite this sleeping area, and on the other side of the main living room, is an attic, which provides more sleeping space and a playroom for the children.

Unusually, the bathroom has been conceived as an inside/outside space. The flooring and walls are lined in timber and the big, old-fashioned, green-painted, roll-top bath sits on a mini-beach of pebbles. It is held in place, like a ship in dry dock, on a pair of substantial wooden cradles. In the summer, after a bath, the owners can step from the bathroom directly outside and into the idyllic landscape to dry off in the warm sun.

← This rustic bathroom, lined with timber flooring and horizontal planked walls, is in a converted barn, now summer house, on the Swedish island of Gotland. The big roll-top bath sits on its own beach of pebbles and is held, ship-like, in a pair of chunky timber cradles.

↓ (left) Simplicity is key to big, open rooms, where walls are bare and washed with pale cream paint, and beams are exposed. The dining chairs are softened with striped, woollen rugs and throws made from Gotland-reared wool.

↓ (right) The children's bedroom has a stone plinth for the bed. The classic rocking horse toy and wooden seagull are in the style of designs by famous Danish designer Kay Bojesen.

noble stone

Owing to the abundance of wood and its comparative ease of use, stone is a building material that is rarely found in contemporary Scandinavian homes. Historically, and for practical reasons, traditional structures (houses and rural buildings such as farmhouses and agricultural buildings) all over the world have always been made from the materials that are to be found in their immediate locality. Through this use of locally found materials, traditional buildings often have the appearance of growing from the landscape, and, as a result, they are in complete aesthetic harmony with their surroundings.

In centuries past there was no construction industry or transportation networks to move building materials easily from location to location. However, where stone was found in plentiful supply it has provided an interesting departure from the more familiar Scandinavian use of wood, or brick as in the case of Denmark. More recently, in Norway there has been a number of interesting small, contemporary summer houses built using huge pebbles as the main building material.

In the house pictured on these pages, huge blocks of roughly hewn local granite have been used in an exciting way in order to create a great monumental backdrop in the living room, while the generous stone hearth is framed in a lighter coloured material. Big, irregularly shaped flagstones have also been used to create the floor in the home office, and there is a more regularly shaped stone floor in the bathroom. The bold use of stone gives the place a powerful rustic air of considerable nobility and substance. The owners of this house have not been tempted to match this feeling with more traditional styles of furniture and furnishings, but instead have furnished it with contemporary furniture to match their modern lifestyle. The contrast in style is exhilarating.

↓ (left) The use of stone is rare in modern Scandinavian homes except where it is available in plentiful supply. Here, by using stone, nature is drawn right inside the bathroom. Underfloor heating ensures that it is warm to the touch.

↓ (right) The big, rustic stone flags sit comfortably with this contemporary style interior. Here, a hi-tech home workstation has been positioned to enjoy the views.

→ The idea that countryside homes have to be traditionally furnished is frequently challenged in Scandinavia. Contemporary furniture, such as this leather chaise longue, looks all the more stylish when set in contrast with a rustic setting.

↑ Tranquillity pervades this Danish turn-of-the century home. The owners, one of whom is interior designer Nanett Nielsson, took their inspiration from homes in Scandinavia, New Mexico, Tuscany, and England. This bedroom occupies what was previously the dining room; the giant bed sits on a raised platform in the window bay.

scandinavian colour palettes

The colour palette for the interiors of most Scandinavian homes is based on a wide range of subtle, neutral colours, and rural homes are no exception to this. Here the gentle, pale tones of cream and ivory move into different shades of stone and grey, then gradually edge toward more earthy pigments. Natural paints such as limewash, distemper, and milk paint, when mixed with natural pigments, produce a luscious, dead-flat matt finish that enhances these colours and looks great in rural dwellings.

Neutral colours were not always used. Visits to older buildings in all of the Nordic countries, particularly historic farmhouses, show interiors painted in rich, dark colours and adorned with a profusion of painted and carved patterns. In Norway, for example, the tradition of folk art produced a form of flower- and pattern-painting called *rosemaling*. This peaked in the late 18th century when the swirling, freehand brushwork was being used to cover just about every surface in the house, including ceilings. Although *rosemaling* translates as "rose painting", it also included intricate, interlocking geometric patterns and pastoral scenes, based on legends and sometimes biblical stories. Many of these traditional, old Scandinavian houses are now preserved as buildings of special historic interest and are open to the public. It was the fresh thinking of the 20th century that influenced a change toward soft, natural, and light-reflecting colours.

These days, while many rural homeowners might keep to a mainly neutral colour palette, the spirit of *rosemaling* is still alive, and they are also not afraid to use colour. Indeed, the exteriors of rural homes in all the Scandinavian countries are often outrageously colourful. For example, in some regions of Norway village houses were, and still sometimes are, painted in different colours. These colours denoted who lived where, and even what their profession was. A house painted white, traditionally the most expensive colour, used to denote a person of stature – perhaps a village elder. The shops and buildings where

↑ (left) The attic space has been opened up to create a generous-sized bathroom, complete with a handsome teak bath tub. Roof lights bring in plenty of sunlight, and ceramic and stone tiling provide an intriguing textural finish to the floor and shower enclosure.

↑ (right) Raised fireplaces are very popular in Scandinavian homes. By placing them higher, the leaping flames can command more attention and become a real focus of the space.

services such as shoe mending were offered, were painted a bright acid yellow. Meanwhile, the dwellings of regular folk were painted a glowing, rich, blood-red – in Sweden, it is called Falun-red and is still used on thousands of rural dwellings. The country house of the famous social reformers and artists Carl and Karin Larsson is a superb example of these colours. The house is traditionally painted Falun-red with white windows, but ochre yellow and sage green are also included. Inside, the place is decorated in a range of colours – yellow for the writing room, cream for Carl's bedroom, and red and green in the dining room.

The use of muted, pale, and subtle colours in Scandinavian interiors is largely for practical reasons – in countries where the sunlight disappears early in the day for at least half of the year it helps to lighten potentially dark and dingy spaces. Pale colours work very effectively as light reflectors, making sure that every scrap of sunlight is bounced around the interior. However, brilliant white, while most effective at light reflection, is not used uniformly in interiors. Often walls that appear to be painted white will actually be offset with a small amount of grey or yellow ochre to produce a softer, more liveable finish. And it is not just the walls that are painted. Timber floors and timber ceilings are also given a wash of white, or off-white, to reflect the precious light upwards or downwards in the room. To achieve a broken colour effect, lime washes and lime paste are applied to wood and then sanded off to reveal the lively pattern of the wood beneath it, but still retaining a lightened effect overall.

↓ The distinctive Polle (meaning Ox in Danish) chair, by the legendary Danish furniture designer Hans Wegner, was designed in 1960. This classic has been chosen by home-owner Morten Broløs, who runs a furniture shop in Arhus, Denmark. The house was designed by Henning Gudnitz.

→ Natural light is a major feature in the Danish home of artist Elsa Sidsner. Designed by architect Adser Schack, the open-plan space also plays with the use of different levels. You step down from the living room into the dining area, which leads directly to the garden. The chairs and the circular table are by the Danish designer Poul Kjærholm.

↑ A palette of neutral colours and natural materials have been elegantly combined here. The crisp bedlinen and woollen blanket sit alongside the sheepskin rug on the floor, and the room is lined with natural pine boarding.

natural, wholesome materials

Rural Scandinavian homes are a celebration of sensuality. Where life is lived close to nature, there is often an innate appreciation of natural materials: the richness and permanence of slate and stone, the warmth and living patterns of woods, and the subtleties of wool, linen, and cottons. Scandinavian style does not attempt to disguise wood under layers of paint, or print fabrics with lavish complex patterns. Instead, there is tremendous honesty in using the materials in a simple, unadorned way and allowing their natural qualities, textures, and grain to be shown to their best advantage. The result of this is the creation of interiors that appear to have grown from their environment, and which are linked directly to it. There is something reassuringly wholesome and even romantic about these rural homes – what could be more appealing, and ecologically sound, than a cosy log cabin or summer house made from the trees that have been felled in the surrounding forest.

The confident handling of raw materials is indicative of cultures that have retained their traditional craft skills. While Scandinavian countries, much like the rest of the Western world, have embraced industry and mass-production, there remains an enviable balance between the use of mechanization to create goods and human input. They have managed to become major exporters of well-made and competitively priced factory-produced goods, including furniture, glassware, ceramics, and textiles, by the creative fusion of man and machine. In Scandinavia, mass-production does not have to mean soulless products.

This sensitivity to raw materials produces interiors where you feel invited to linger: living rooms where you want to sink into softly upholstered chairs and sofas as you relax in front of a real log fire, and bedrooms where, at the end of the day, you can sleep in a luxurious bed dressed in linen and woollen blankets. This particularly applies to rural homes, where the outside environment can be wild and relatively unspoiled by the interventions of humans; where long, cold winters make day-to-day life difficult and occasionally hostile, here the comfort of the home is highly prized.

Although the palette of materials and colours is often restrained, the skill in combining them in subtle ways has become a hallmark of Scandinavian style. When the brilliant pioneers such as Alvar Aalto and Arne Jacobsen had their imaginations fired by the likes of the Bauhaus, Le Corbusier, and Mies van der Rohe, they embraced the ideas of fresh, simple spaces and gave them a Scandinavian interpretation. Alvar Aalto saw the thrilling, modern, gravity-defying tubular steel furniture created by great names such as Marcel Breuer and Walter Groupius, and then made his own version. Cold steel was no material for a freezing Finnish climate, so he created his own interpretations, replacing the steel with warm wood. By employing a method of steaming the wood he bent and formed it into soft, sensual shapes – one of the earliest examples is the still modern-looking chair he designed in the early 1930s for the Paimio Sanatorium. Held within the bent wood frame is a single curved sheet of plywood, designed so that patients could sit upright and breathe comfortably. Arne Jacobsen also experimented with various techniques for moulding plywood into figure-hugging chair seats. He then took sculptural forms a stage further with his organic-shaped Egg and Swan chairs, which he designed for the SAS Royal Hotel in Copenhagen. The tactile qualities of natural material and human-friendly shapes continue to be themes that are explored by Scandinavian designers today.

↓ Candlelight has been arranged with great care in this rural Swedish home. One particularly appealing idea is the use of tea-light candles to mark every step of the stairway.

← Huge floor-to-ceiling sheets of glass draw in lots of natural light and offer great views in this Japanese-inspired home by Danish industrial designer Ole Palsby. The blue thermal jug on the table is called Classic No 1, and was designed by Palsby in 1985 for the Danish manufacturer Alfi. The 1956 plywood and leather Lounge Chair is by American designers Charles and Ray Eames.

↑ Located in North Zealand, Denmark, the house was conceived to be transparent so that the inside and the outside were linked. The raised studio area has fantastic views, and also serves as a shelter for the log store below.

← The entrance of the house is sheltered and welcoming, with views piercing the house, through the horizontal windows above the kitchen worksurface, and back outside. The kitchen system, called Connections, was designed by Ole Palsby for the Danish manufacturer Kvik, and the green chairs are by Charles and Ray Eames.

rural retreat – serjø bay, denmark

For more than a decade the family of internationally renowned Danish architect and industrial designer Knud Holscher has owned a post-war summer house, situated about an hour's drive from Copenhagen. It is here that the family spend their weekends and holidays, in a friendly and comfortable building that was made at the end of the war from the scarce materials that were available at that time. These materials included recycled timbers and second-hand windows and doors. "But with three children growing into adults, the space seemed to get smaller and smaller. So much so that we felt we had to spend all our time outside," explains Knud Holscher, who began his career with design legend and fellow Dane, Arne Jacobsen. He worked with Jacobsen on the highly praised St Catherine's College in Oxford, England and has subsequently designed such prestigious buildings as the Royal Danish Theatre in Copenhagen, Copenhagen Airport, and a number

↓ Located in Serjø Bay, one hour's drive north of Copenhagen, this single, uninterrupted, multi-functional space was designed by internationally renowned Danish architect and designer Knud Holscher as his own weekend and holiday hideaway. The only enclosed area is the bathroom, which is located behind the curved wall. Almost all the furniture was designed by the Finnish master Alvar Aalto.

↑ The space and furnishings are undeniably contemporary in style, but there is a permanent reminder of the rural setting with the views, and the rough-hewn timber columns that were found in a Copenhagen salvage yard.

of houses in the Middle East. In addition to these high-profile architectural projects, Holscher has also worked on a vast range of industrial products, including the ultra-sleek and multiple-award-winning d-line range of stainless steel door furniture. Today, Knud Holscher Industrial Design is one of Scandinavia's best-known design companies.

When the time came to create the much-needed extra space in the summer house Holscher's solution was to design a delicate, light-filled, open-plan cabin intended to be just for the parents, with the children continuing to use the old summer house. This was permitted by the Danish planning laws, which allowed the possibility of building an additional one-storey building in the grounds of the existing family summer house.

The simple, rectangular, single-storey building that Holscher created has a gently barrel-vaulted roof, which cleverly adds height, interest, and softness to the interior. From the outside, the curved form also has the effect of dissolving any sense of bulkiness as a

↑ This wide timber deck catches the sun perfectly, but if things get too hot shelter can be sought in the shadows cast by the deep eaves.

→ Leading in from the deck outside is the bedroom. The large bed on wheels is a prototype designed by Knud Holscher. The sliding headrest is ideal for sitting up and reading in bed and the cantilevered shelf acts as a clever alternative to a bedside table. The only separation between the sleeping area and the main living space is the serpentine screen designed by Finnish architect Alvar Aalto.

pitched roof would have been a far more intrusive feature in the landscape. Undeterred by some comments, Holscher adds "I've heard all the jokes about it looking like a badminton hall inside, but it really doesn't bother me".

The home is built with local fir wood, both inside and out. The curved roof is finished on the outside with roofing felt. The roof is held in place, with great delicacy, on 10mm (0.4in) steel plates that sit on top of rough-hewn square posts. These are set at regular intervals on both sides of the house, and in a single row through the middle of the house. The rustic-style posts were found in a Copenhagen salvage yard. To enclose the space, the entire building is wrapped all the way around with huge expanses of glass. Although the house is in an entirely secluded location, there is the option of drawing down Venetian blinds for privacy, or for protection from intense summer sun. The whole effect is one of delicacy and transparency, and it has an almost pavilion or even canvas marquee feel about it. As would be expected of Holscher, the finishes are simple, practical, and robust. "I've whitewashed the floor to achieve that pale, grey colour," he explains. The ceiling is lined with sheets of inexpensive birch ply that has been washed with a mix of calcium and soap in order to achieve a matching pale grey tone. For those lazy summer days, the house is surrounded by the all-important Scandinavian timber sunbathing deck.

The interior of the cabin is a single, free-flowing space – "I don't like corridors," says Holscher. The sleeping space is at one end, and there is a kitchen and dining area at the other. The kitchen is constructed from a standard Scandinavian kitchen system, and, to reduce its impact on the room, half of the units and shelving are set back into a recess in the end wall. An island counter separates the kitchen from the rest of the room, and the whole area is bathed in the natural light that falls through a large skylight in the roof. The only separate room, the bathroom, is located in the centre of the cabin and is enclosed by a curved, solid wall, not quite ceiling height and finished in grey. On the outside of the curve, which echoes the shape of the roof, is set a large fireplace.

At the sleeping end of the space sits a Kund Holscher-designed prototype bed. The wooden base is held off the ground on wheels, and it features a sliding, well-padded headrest, perfect for sitting up and reading in bed. There is also a cantilevered shelf, which is ideal for books or a glass or teacup. The bed is separated from the living area by a curved wooden screen, designed by the famous Finnish architecture hero Alvar Aalto. "In fact just about all the furniture in the place is by Aalto," explains Holscher. "I happened to be visiting Helsinki when the showroom was having a great sale, so I bought a whole collection of items." His impressive haul includes the familiar Model 100 serpentine screen, from 1935; Stool 60, the three-legged birch stool designed in 1933 and featuring Aalto's ingenious curved-leg form; the Tea Trolley 901, designed in 1936; a pair of cantilevered armchairs, from 1933, that feature a moulded and laminated birch wood frame; and a pair of chaise longue, called Lounge Chair 43, with upholstery in cream webbing, designed in 1937. On the dining table and trolley is one of the best-known Scandinavian design icons – the wobbly shaped, glass Savoy vase from 1936, which was designed by Aalto for the Savoy restaurant in Helsinki. This restaurant is a great place to visit, as the Aalto-designed interior is perfectly preserved and looks just as it did when it was first created by him in 1936.

→ The dining chairs here, designed in 1949 by the Danish designer Hans Wegner, are called Round chairs. At the height of the American fascination with Scandinavian Modern design, 12 of them were ordered by a US Television station for the 1960 televised live debate between John F. Kennedy and Richard Nixon.

↑ From the main living area of the house, steps lead down to a spacious kitchen and dining area that is set at the same level as the garden. One huge, vertical window frames the tall trees in the landscape beyond.

→ Danish architect Lars Nymand has added drama to the space by opening up the ceiling area to the roof, where skylights allow sunlight to pour in. The dark wood of the floor is echoed in the dark wood of the chopping block.

↑ This contemporary interpretation of the log cabin was designed jointly by the Swedish architecture practices Sandell Sandberg and Landström Arkitekter. It incorporates the simplicity of the traditional log cabin while adding a modern twist with contemporary furniture and ecological features, such as a super-efficient underfloor heating system.

the nest – northern sweden

The log cabin has, for generations, been a style of building that many Scandinavians love and feel extremely comfortable with. It is easy and inexpensive to build, uses local, sustainable materials, and blends in well with the surrounding landscape. On the down side, traditional log-cabin design has tended to lack innovation and excitement. However, as a result it has become a building type that numerous architects and designers have relished the opportunity to experiment with.

Among the most recent essays in reinvention is a design called Vistet, which means "nest" in Swedish. The house was commissioned by the local government of northern Sweden, and the design ideas were conceived by a collaboration of two high-profile young architecture practices, Sandell Sandberg and Landström Arkitekter. It is an extremely adaptable design – in the larger form it is suitable as a family home, while in a smaller version it is perfect as a summer holiday house.

"We looked back to traditional buildings, the log cabins made using round logs, and to farmhouses," explains architect Thomas Sandell. For Vistet, round logs were replaced with sawn pine wood – a building material in plentiful supply in Sweden. "Inside, the space was divided into two areas, just like traditional farmhouses, one large living space, and a second space for hallways, stairs, and storage." The traditional open-plan living space has a kitchen and dining area at one end and a comfortable seating area at the other. In the middle of the house is a large and efficient wood-burning fire that is raised up the wall, off the ground, to improve heat dispersion. Sandell continues: "The idea is that the large kitchen/dining and living space is kept warm at normal room temperature with the help of energy-efficient underfloor heating, but the second space is much cooler. This represents savings on fuel bills." Indeed, so ecological was the design that it won Sweden's first ever ecological certification from the World Wildlife Foundation.

↑ (left) As well as looking to log cabins for their inspiration, the architects also took some ideas from traditional Swedish farmhouses that are designed in two sections, one warm for living in and one cool for storage. Here, the open-plan living room is kept warm, while areas such as the hall, stairs, and storage spaces are kept cool.

↑ (right) The simple Swedish pine-built home has a welcoming entrance framed by a pair of built-in benches, ideal for sitting on in good weather, and for acting as a shelter in bad weather.

↑ Built in 1877, this Danish house has been remodelled and opened up by architect Maj-britt Hou-Vangsaae. The drama of the big double-height living spaces is echoed in the eye-catching, dramatic roofscape. Exciting geometric shapes in this house include a large circular window.

letting light into the home

The contemporary Scandinavian home is a place where natural sunlight is encouraged and welcomed, almost worshipped. When the weather is warm, doors and windows are flung wide open to bring the outside in. When the weather is cool, the generous windows let in light and conquer any feelings of being held hostage by the cold.

In the past, many rural homes were built with great thick walls and tiny windows, in order to provide protection from the onslaught of long winters. These were introverted buildings, often huddled close together for protection from the sharp winds that are blown off the North Sea and the bone-chilling Baltic blasts. Where they stood apart from their neighbours, homes hunkered down in the landscape to escape the worst of the prevailing winds. However, by the start of the 20th century modern glass manufacturing processes made it possible to produce huge panels of plate glass, and Scandinavian designers were quick to embrace the possibilities this offered. One of the key characteristics of 20th-century Scandinavian design became large windows, giving homes an extrovert appearance; here was the opportunity to enjoy great views and to invite in as much feel-good sunlight as possible. In the classic summer houses of the 1940s, '50s, and '60s, the idea of openness began to be explored with relish – big plate-glass windows were accompanied by large sliding or folding doors, which allowed the homes to be opened up fully to nature. In these places, concerns about insulation and warmth were rarely important as the houses were used, and continue to be used, only during the warm summer months.

In the case of permanent homes, the need for winter warmth was afforded a higher priority, and builders were among the first to pioneer modern ideas such as double glazing, and now triple glazing, to provide insulation from the cold. Wood-framed,

Scandinavian-designed windows have since set world standards for energy efficiency and are a major export, being the window of choice for many designers of ecological homes.

More recent innovations in glass production have included intelligent materials where an invisible coating allows light and warmth to flow inside the home and prevents heat from escaping. The idea of internal windows has also gained currency. In order to draw natural light right into the very heart of the home, windows are punched into internal walls, often at high levels, allowing the light to flow right through the house into every room. With regards to window dressings, they too remain in keeping with the simple and uncluttered style of Scandinavian interiors. Windows are rarely fussily dressed with curtains, and instead are either hung with fine muslin or Venetian blinds, or even left entirely free from any obstructions that might block out the precious sun.

It is also interesting to note the large number of Scandinavian manufacturers that make beautiful lamps and light fittings in order to fulfil the need to supplement natural light and to lift the spirits. Great names like Artek and Louis Poulsen are among those making the classic designs created by Arne Jacobsen, Alvar Aalto, and Poul Henningsen. Henningsen's famous PH lamps, which he began to design in the 1920s, were among the first modern-style lighting designs. Distinctively flower-like, they are composed of layers of shades and fins, which cleverly soften and reflect the light that is emitted by a naked bulb. More recently these names have been joined by contemporary designers, including the Finn Brita Flander. She has had a long fascination with the Finnish relationship with light and darkness, and has taken her inspiration from the past by reinventing, in numerous contemporary ways, the traditional *päre*. The *päre* is a stick of resinous fir wood that burns with a bright flame, and traditionally was used by rural communities in place of candles.

← Inside, exciting spaces are created using unusually angled walls. Here, the internal wall leads the eye through the space and into the landscape beyond. A splash of colour is introduced into the otherwise neutral setting using a large painting.

↓ (left) Glass, set into the top of these tall walls, enables light to flow through the entire house. A contemporary style, stainless steel-framed fireplace, set into a large chimney piece, forms a central hub to the home.

↓ (right) In Scandinavian countries awareness of design and colour schemes is introduced to the very young. In this children's bedroom are child-size versions of the famous, moulded ply-wood Ant chair by Danish designer Arne Jacobsen.

contemporary home – ärhus, denmark

Having lovingly restored and lived in an old farmhouse nearby, the Danish family that commissioned this contemporary home was ready for a complete change. "The old farmhouse was absolutely traditional and picturesque, and had the wonderful feeling of coziness, which people, particularly in Denmark, find so enjoyable," explains the architect Claus Hermansen. "It was typical of its type, introverted, cosy, and actually sheltering from nature. But this busy, cosmopolitan family likes a challenge and decided that their new house, 10 km (6¼ miles) south of Ärhus, the second-largest city in Denmark, should be the complete opposite. They wanted large open spaces, plenty of light, areas where family life and business sometimes mix, interaction with the near landscape, and plenty of views."

New building in the Danish countryside is closely regulated, so the house design had to be "traditional" enough to win the approval of the planning authorities, while also satisfying the family's need for contemporary living. Inspiration for the project was therefore taken directly from the surrounding traditional rural architecture. The house is built from cedar wood, brick, concrete, galvanized steel, and slate, and incorporates modest detailing such as a traditional pitched roof. It is also respectful of the natural surroundings. Says Hermansen: "It had to be a design that would blend in with nature and look as if it was growing out of the landscape, while also being built from strong materials. Like farm buildings it was relatively inexpensive to build, and is able to cope with rough weather."

The result is a strikingly modern design with the simplicity of a child's drawing. Although built from traditional materials, it is unmistakably of the 21st century. Inside, the space is turned upside down, with the bedrooms and quiet rooms downstairs in a partially buried brick-built wing, which helps to shelter the house from strong winds. The large first-floor room provides a generous, sunny living space with fantastic views.

↓ Designed by architect Claus Hermansen, this home has taken inspiration from traditional barn designs. By turning the interior upside down, the bedrooms have been moved to ground level and the living space is elevated to the first floor, where the owners can enjoy views over the gentle rural landscape.

→ The open-plan first floor living space makes the most of views and also sunlight. The sense of space is enhanced by having the room open to the very apex of the roof. The colour scheme is based on neutral creams and stone tones.

↑ In tune with the grand scale of these rooms, the island kitchen has an almost monumental look to it. The open-plan interior is given added interest with the use of different floor levels — the kitchen sits on a plinth reached by a broad flight of stairs from the living area.

in harmony with nature

Many people think of Scandinavian countries as being blessed with huge, wide-open tracts of countryside, which, of course, they are, but this does not mean that the building of new homes is taken lightly or that the regulations governing it are in any way easy. In the Nordic countries, contemporary rural homes must be built with considerable sensitivity to their natural surroundings and, as in most Western countries, strict planning laws govern all aspects of new building. Often architects are required to submit plans that use the local design language – for example, in many areas the traditional pitched roof is preferred over flat or even barrel-vaulted shapes. Those designers who want to depart from the traditional norm must prepare themselves for lengthy negotiations with extremely cautious planning authorities. As well as style, there are usually controls that govern the height of new buildings, and planners will also certainly want to keep a tight rein on the types of materials that are used in construction. Although the process can be fraught with frustration, this conservative approach is the main reason that so much of the rural landscape remains intact and unscarred by new building.

As well as having a rather careful and cautious approach to planning buildings, Scandinavia has also become synonymous with the best in ecological design, building materials, and construction techniques. Perhaps due to their unbroken contact with nature, architects and designers in these countries were among the first to recognize that constructing new buildings could be achieved in a way that was more sensitive to the environment. For example, in designing many new homes the path of the sun and direction of the cold winds are taken into consideration, together with the surrounding landscape and natural features such as trees and rocks. The orientation of a house is most important when working with nature – the most sensitively designed homes are positioned with their back to the oncoming harsh weather. Walls that face the bad weather are solid, well-insulated,

↓ This imposing country house is set on a hillside and is designed to take advantage of the amazing views that surround it. The living room is the part of the house that is closest to the view, and is made almost entirely of glass. The remaining parts, set further back, are made in more solid materials.

and have small windows. In some cases buildings are sunk into the ground, and the earth is used as a protective buffer to shelter them against the prevailing winds. The warmer, sunnier, south side of buildings, meanwhile, often feature large areas of glass that open up the houses to the precious sunlight. With the latest developments in glass manufacture, the glazing used here can be coated to help regulate the internal temperature. Systems using low-emissivity glass work in a similar way to a Thermos flask, by keeping the interior at a stable temperature – warm in winter and cool in summer.

In considering a potential site, any housebuilder will acknowledge that a flat plateau provides an easy base on which to build. However, the challenge of an undulating plot, or even a steep hillside, can also produce some extremely exciting results. Instead of fighting with the problem and attempting to flatten out a sloping site, at considerable extra cost, many new homes in Scandinavia are being designed with a more sensitive approach to the landscape. More and more, architects are finding ways to make buildings fit into their environment, to hug the contours, or to stand on pillars and float above the craggy boulders, which may have been there for millions of years. In a handful of examples, homes have even been designed around living nature. One of the most successful and startling is the Johnsen Summer House (*see* page 26) by the Norwegian architect Carl-Viggo Hølmebakk. In this case he used computer mapping to fit the building around a small stand of trees, which were left to grow up and through the building, providing a spectacular, natural feature.

In terms of materials and construction, homes are built using what is locally available, where possible. Timber is the most widely used, and has been demonstrated to be thoroughly sustainable. Denmark and Sweden continue to be world leaders in producing extremely high-quality and stylish, double- and triple-glazed windows, which are the first choice in countless environmentally sound housebuilding projects around the world. Their high levels of wall- and roof-insulation have also been setting global standards for decades.

↓ The farmhouse and barn aesthetic has provided inspiration to generations of modern architects. Here, Finnish architect Juha Paldanius has combined timber with huge areas of glass. The living area has been raised to the first floor, where there is a greater fall of sunlight.

↑ A dynamic mixture of assymetrical spaces has gone into making up this very unusual hilltop home, designed by Finnish architect Jyrki Tasa. The house incorporates a range of materials including concrete, steel, and timber.

scandinavian wood finishes

The warm, sensual, and decorative qualities of wood are powerful features in many contemporary interiors. It is not unusual for wood to be used in an untreated state that shows off its beautiful grain, patterns, and natural colourings. It can even be used in hardwearing areas, such as flooring, and be allowed to acquire its own patina through age, cleaning, and use. Scandinavian designers are particularly well-known for their creative use of a huge variety of woods to achieve different decorative effects and finishes that can withstand the wear and tear of everyday life.

The Finnish architect Yrjö Suonto is among a band of contemporary architects who are concerned with creating environmentally-sound homes (*see* the project pictured left). Among his most recent experiments has been his work with a material called thermo wood – birch wood that has been oven-baked to give it the richly coloured appearance of a tropical hardwood. The process itself can be carefully controlled in order to bake the wood to different shades, from a pale biscuit colour through to a dark brown. The heat also gives the material extra strength. The dining table and chairs, shown left, have been built using thermo wood, and have been waxed to produce a lustrous finish, which shows off the grain pattern. This process is being hailed as extremely environmentally sound, because using this type of wood means that the material can be sourced locally, thus reducing demand on the world's stock of precious, and often rare, exotic hardwoods.

Oils and waxes are used in many different ways in Scandinavian homes to achieve different finishes. Products, including Danish oil, finishing oil, and tung oil, are made from a blend of natural oils and resins. As they soak into the surface of the wood they emphasize the grain patterns, and, when exposed to the air, they also set hard, forming a durable, protective layer. The result of using such products is a subtle satin finish, which is good for shelving, floors with fairly low foot-traffic, and worksurfaces. Many are even suitable for kitchen worktops, although manufacturer's instructions should be checked first to confirm that they are safe to use where food is being prepared. As well as looking fantastic, these products have the advantage of being made of natural materials, they have a fairly low odour, and they help to prevent infestations of beetles and bugs. Wood soap is another product that is used regularly. Again, it produces a lustrous finish but is not as tough as either varnish or lacquer. Although waxes and linseed oil soak into the wood surface and produce a rich sheen finish, they do not set hard, so, while they create a water-resistant finish, they are not durable and do not protect the wood from knocks and dents. When it comes to adding super-tough finishes for floors in areas like hallways or kitchens, varnish is often preferred because of its durability.

Clear and colourless waxes, oils, and varnishes are extremely popular with many Scandinavian designers, and in addition they often make use of wood stains to add depth and colour to the wood they are working with. Wood stains are colour pigments that are suspended in a clear liquid, either water or white spirit. The liquid penetrates the wood surface with the pigments so that, when it dries, the natural grain pattern remains visible, but there is also a glow of warm background colour. Very occasionally, wooden floors may be given a solid, painted coating. This is often in white, and is used by designers as a way of brightening up a dark interior by reflecting light.

← This room is a celebration of wood. The furniture and objects demonstrate the tremendous ingenuity and skills that are still used in Scandinavian countries. There has been an unbroken tradition for centuries in these countries of working with wood of all sorts.

↓ An elegant and contemporary space by Finnish designer Sebastian Lönnqvist. As in many Scandinavian interiors, the wood-burning stove is at the heart of a very tall room. Furnishings include the famous wood trolley by Alvar Aalto.

the red house – near oslo, norway

There is an unmistakable air of excitement about The Red House. It could be mistaken for a military border post or an amazing contemporary restaurant, but it is, in fact, an incredible rural home – the dazzlingly innovative work of the Norwegian architecture practice Jarmund/Vigsnæs. The scarlet flat-top box, with its distinctive horizontal ribbon of windows that wrap around the circumference of the building, is dug into an extremely steep, south-facing, forested hillside not too far from the western suburbs of Oslo.

"The house design grew from the story of its location and its owners," explains Einar Jarmund who, when describing his projects, often infuses them with a scenic or even filmic storyline. "One of the owners had been brought up in an older big house, just up the hill. When the family sold up, this land (the former garden) was kept as a potential building plot. So the long, low, flat-roof shape of the building was dictated by the fact that it shouldn't spoil the view of the valley from the older house. And just like others locally, it is built with common materials – it is a timber house with timber cladding."

Nearby homes were mostly built in the 1930s as Oslo expanded during a small building boom. It might have been possible to build at least half a dozen homes on a plot of this size, but Norwegian sensibilities – the desire for space, solitude, and distance from neighbours – prevailed, and ensured that just one home was built. In Norway, land for new homes close to the major population centres is becoming increasingly hard to find. Where building plots do occur they are often on difficult terrain, such as the steep slope on which The Red House is built. "Around perhaps 50 years ago, you could choose where you wanted to build a house, all the best spots are now gone. So nowadays many sites are marginal, but for us that is not a problem," says Jarmund. "The difficulty creates an interesting challenge. Here the steepness of the hillside makes the house more intriguing. In the end it makes our job a lot more interesting than working with a perfect site."

The interior planning is upside down – the bedrooms and ancillary spaces are downstairs and face the river valley to the north, while the large, open-plan living space is upstairs and is oriented south – the view creating the internal "terrace" that was requested by the clients. Here, views of nature in the raw can be enjoyed. The interior is contemporary in style and bathed with light, drawn in through the great horizontal band of glass that runs around the entire building. To ensure that the views are uninterrupted the architects have pulled the structural supports for the roof back into the internal space, leaving the band of glass to stand alone and undisturbed.

While the living space is largely open-plan, there are several quiet, more secluded areas. These are divided from the main social area by the use of chest-height walls that enclose the softer areas containing sofas and chairs. The owners had no interest in surrounding their home with a cultivated garden, and instead wanted the house to act as its own terrace within the landscape. It is possible to hear the stream that runs along the bottom of the valley when approaching the house, or out walking nearby.

Finally, the eye-catching red colour is a key part of the story. The area itself has red in its name, as does the client's name, and the other houses in the area have also been painted in a variety of colours, although none so brilliant as this. "Also, it reflects the client's temperament," adds Jarmund.

↑ Appropriately enough for a home called The Red House, the neutral backdrop of the interior has been enlivened by bold splashes of red. The sofa, with its chest-height screen wall, makes a cosy seating area, marked off from the open-plan space of the rest of the interior.

→ The ingenious design here has set the structural supports back from the outer edge of the house, thus enabling an unbroken horizontal ribbon of window to run the length of the space. The wide window ledge is a superb place to pause and take in the Norwegian forest outside.

↓ (Overleaf) This space, by Norwegian architects Div. A, with its long refectory-style dining table and benches, is almost monastic in its simplicity. Clever and practical details include the raised-up fireplace on the left, with its handy log store below, and the deep window seats on the right.

rural innovation

In most countries around the world, the most adventurous, cutting-edge home design is to be found in urban areas; this is not true of Scandinavian countries. Where there are enlightened clients and adventurous architects, large numbers of rural homes continue to foster the Scandinavian pioneering spirit of design that emerged in the early 20th century. With every new building there is the opportunity to try out fresh ideas and to reinvent the great building types of the past – the farmhouses, fishermen's huts, summer houses, labourers' cottages, and woodland log cabins. Many designers choose to acknowledge the age-old skills and building traditions that have been used for centuries. They are able also to move the story on, and to incorporate the best new thinking and latest technology in order to make appealing contemporary homes.

The most innovative recent designs tackle areas such as space engineering – creating new ways of living in an age where work and family life have become less clearly defined – and so providing home offices and space for visiting clients within the family home. Many have turned the traditional home upside down, making the most of the naturally lit upper floors for large, open-plan living and putting the bedrooms on lower levels.

In Scandinavian countries there is always a concern for the environment, from the way a building sits in the landscape to its impressive insulation levels and efficient use of energy. In many cases, locally available building materials are used, but they may be deployed in new ways or occasionally combined with steel and concrete to add excitement or drama. There continues to be a prolific use of wood, but where, in the past, it may have been painted or stained dark, it is now used in its natural state, usually light in colour, and in refined and elegant ways. Above all comes the delight and skill in making comfortable, sensual, practical, warm, well-lit, and welcoming contemporary homes.

↓ (left) The proximity to nature is enjoyed in many Scandinavian homes. The big sliding glass doors on both sides of this corner post open up the living room to the terrace outside.

↓ (right) This must be about as close as it gets to recreating a sense of sleeping in the forest. The bed is surrounded completely by a "tent" of fresh-smelling wooden boards.

→ While contemporary Scandinavian homes almost always incorporate huge windows, many also feature ingenious additional ways to bring sunlight inside. Here, in this pale wood interior, a triangular panel of glass has been inserted into the gable end of the home.

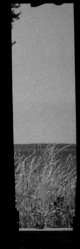

waterside

elemental inspiration

From the fjords of Norway to the spectacular lakelands of Finland, the vast sandy beaches of Denmark to the delightful Stockholm archipelago, Scandinavia's rivers, waterways, and coastlines are remarkable features of the landscape. For centuries fishing and seafaring have provided essential incomes for the people who have built their sturdy but simple homes and communities close to the water's edge. Locations that were originally chosen for convenience by those who made their living from the water are nowadays highly prized for their fantastic and inspiring views.

To get an idea of the scale and impact that water has on Scandinavian countries you need only to look at their geographical profiles. Denmark has around 7,300km (4,500 miles) of coastline in a country with a population of little more than five million people. Finland, with a similar-sized population, has a coastline of 4,400km (2,760 miles) and contains some 187,000 lakes, making it the largest lake region in Europe. Sweden, with a population of almost nine million, boats a coastline of 2,400km (1,500 miles) and over 90,000 lakes, while Norway, with its population of around four-and-a-half million residents, has an astonishingly long coastline, including fjords, which measures some 25,000km (15,500 miles).

With all this water surrounding them, it is not surprising that there are so many Scandinavian folk tales based on the sea. There is also an enduring fascination with the Vikings. Their navigational skills and warmongering resulted in a massive expansion of the Danish empire, the "united Danish kingdom", to include parts of what are now Germany, Sweden, Norway, and England. The ancient, intricately woven, decorative patterns that were found on Viking artifacts and textiles became an important part of house decoration at the end of the 1800s.

Since steam boats and trains opened up the landscape to tourists, holiday-home owners, and commuters, there has been a steady growth of building in the prime waterside locations – a trip through the Stockholm archipelago, or along any Scandinavian river, will soon reveal the extent of this. In some places individual homes are scattered across the landscape, while elsewhere purpose-built holiday complexes and resorts have been created. The fabulously pretty thatched beach houses, which sit among the soft dunes of the western coast of Jutland in Denmark, are fine examples of how structures, both new and old, can be designed and built to sit comfortably in a landscape of such outstanding natural beauty.

← It is hard to beat the Stockholm archipelago in Sweden for tranquil and beautiful waterside locations. The sunny, yellow Villa Honkala is typical of the many late 19th- and early 20th-century homes that were built in this area.

→ For that perfect "get-away-from-it all" feeling, the rugged Swedish coatline provides the perfect spot for this modern, timber-built summer house by architect Anders Landström.

← Leo Henriksen's house was designed in 1956 by Arne Jacobsen. More than half of the exterior is clad in glass, with steel panels, and, where there are views of the garden, the living room is wrapped entirely in floor-to-ceiling glass. To the right of the house is the owner's sculptural, brick-built, herring smokehouse, designed by Jacobsen in 1943.

a new way of living – arne jacobsen

In the early decades of the 20th century, with the surge of interest in healthy waterside living and the growth of holidays and tourism, architects grasped the opportunity to design in new and modern ways that responded to natural settings. In the first few years of his career, the Danish architect Arne Jacobsen was among the pioneers of this fresh International Style. He achieved early recognition in the late 1920s by winning a competition for the design of the House of the Future. Completed with colleague Flemming Lassen, this electrifying, circular modern house came complete with mooring for a motorboat, a garage, and a landing pad for an autogyra – a futuristic mini helicopter.

The house was built and put on show at the 1929 Architects' Building and Housing Exhibition in Copenhagen – at that time the largest show of its kind ever seen in Scandinavia – and it quickly captured imaginations. The constant stream of visitors loved the radical drum shape, the well-lit interiors, and the inside-outside sun terrace. While it was never built for a real client, Jacobsen revisited the idea in the 1950s when working for Leo Henriksen. He had already completed one commission in the 1940s for Henriksen – a herring smokehouse close to the coast at Odden Harbour, Denmark. The brick-built, whitewashed building, with its trio of monumental chimneys, remains a Jacobsen gem.

Set back from this building was the plot for Henriksen's new home. Already in place was a wavy, serpentine hedge, which gave the new house some shelter. To protect the owners from curious sightseers, the back of the home is clad in white metal panels separated by vertical slits of glass; the more secluded side is finished in floor-to-ceiling glass.

However, Jacobsen's waterside building did not stop at luxurious and experimental one-off designs, as he also designed the stunning neighbouring seaside resorts of Bellevue and Bellavista at Klampenborg (see page 78), a few kilometres north of Copenhagen. Hot on the heels of his success with the House of the Future, work began on the resorts in 1930 and continued for much of the decade. Clearly influenced by Le Corbusier and the Bauhaus school, the designs were simple and functional. Jacobsen designed in the white International Style, working on everything from a crescent of white, low-rise apartments, each with a sea-view balcony, to a theatre, a restaurant, beach-based changing huts, a snack kiosk, and even the paper cups for ice cream.

In the mid-1940s Jacobsen returned to Klampenborg, this time to build a number of modest terrace houses, one of which he kept for himself and lived in until his death in 1971. Klampenborg remains a popular seaside resort and the restaurant there has now been named "Jacobsen" in his honour.

→ This exciting plan for the House of the Future launched Jacobsen's career in 1929. The competition-winning design drew huge crowds when it was built at the 1929 Architects' Building and Housing Exhibition in Copenhagen. Along with housing a car port and boat mooring, the flat roof of the house was intended as a landing pad for the autogyra – a futuristic small helicopter.

→ This sublimely elegant, timber sun terrace
was built as part of a sauna complex by Finnish
architect Aarno Ruusuvuori in the 1960s. With
its integral bench seat, this neat cube of outdoor
space is pushed out through a thicket of marshy
grasses at the water's edge to give spectacular
views of the huge lake.

↓ The simple interior of this summer house
is perfect as a weekend and holiday retreat.
To keep the space clean and uncluttered,
storage space is provided in walls lined with
sheer-fronted cupboards. As a reminder of the
rural setting, rush matting is used on the floor.

inspiration from the past

The very earliest waterside homes to be found in Scandinavia were discovered during excavations in Denmark. The Viking fortress of Trelleborg, next to the water on the west coast of Zealand (the island on which Copenhagen lies), dates from around AD 1000. The encampment was surrounded by a huge circular embankment of earth, and its walls were once fortified with oak planks. Taking their inspiration from the architecture of the ship, the long houses inside this wood-clad ring were almost 31m (100ft) in length, with roofs that bore a striking resemblance to upturned boats. Each house would have been inhabited by up to 50 people. Since its discovery, excavations have shown that the fortress included 16 of these long houses, laid out in a pattern of four blocks of four homes. Each set of four homes were placed to form a square. A reconstruction of one of these homes shows how the huge, upturned hull of a roof is set on rows of columns, which circle the building like a ship's balustrade. This discovery has provided evidence that, even many hundreds of years ago, there was a strong link between home and boat in Scandinavia.

Today it is still possible to draw parallels between the structure of a boat and the architecture of so many Scandinavian waterside homes. Most of the buildings are wooden, often there is a surrounding timber deck, and in many cases there is a look-out point or balcony. The interiors are often furnished with an abundance of neat, built-in furniture and cupboards. In the same way that rural houses succeed in uniting the inside with the outside, so too do waterside homes. They also include elements borrowed from boats, such as stainless steel tension wires for restraining the structure, sheets of canvas to provide shade, and even pontoons that stretch out over the water.

The Finnish home and sauna pictured here were designed by architect Aarno Ruusuvuori in 1966 and they echo the maritime theme. Built at Bökars in Porvoo, the house is a simple, wood-built structure, which features a sheltered outdoor deck, cantilevered over marshy grasses with spectacular views of the water. The home was commissioned by the textile and fashion house Marimekko, and designed and built as an experimental home. The original idea was to explore new methods of prefabricated building, so this rectangular space was built using a series of ready-made panels. Similar to any boat, the interior is lined with in-built cupboards, and the galley-style kitchen has been reduced to just the bare essentials.

national characteristics

When people think of Scandinavia it's often tempting to imagine it as a single entity, a single country even. Many see it as a fairly homogenous region of wide open spaces, forests, lakes, streams, and tall, blonde-haired people creating rational, modern design. However, this is a very broad generalization. Although they do share some characteristics, each country has its own geographic, social, cultural, and economic story.

It is worthwhile looking at how different landscapes, cultures, raw materials, skills, and strands of Nordic heritage have produced nations with individual ways of looking at and practising design and creating the ideal home. Any attempt at generalizing a nation is open to criticism, but there are traits that few would dispute.

Norway, in terms of contemporary design, is often put to one side. It has an air of introversion and has certainly suffered from not having a great 20th-century pioneering architect or designer similar in stature to Arne Jacobsen in Denmark, or Alvar Aalto in Finland. Norway is most often associated with folk culture, traditional textiles, and comfortable but folksy homes, but this stereotype is just part of the truth. Norwegian design has always included a band of architects and designers interested in the avant-garde and in solving problems with logical, well-crafted solutions. Their work in ergonomic and ecologically driven design, particularly furniture, is world class.

Finland has a more quirky, outward-going nature. The country embraced Modernism early in the 20th century, and focused on the production of high-quality but contemporary everyday objects, such as tableware, glassware, ceramics, metal products, textiles, furniture, and sports and leisure goods. Inspiring designers have long been employed by manufacturers to ensure quality and innovation, giving equal weight to utility and aesthetics.

Swedish design is confident and rational, always with a human touch, putting people and user-friendliness to the forefront. Like all other Scandinavian countries, Sweden has a highly developed social vision and has done more than most to research and advance the production of high-quality housing.

Finally, Denmark. The Danes have excelled in the design and production of extremely high-quality, innovative, contemporary furniture and products. Ecological and ergonomic concerns are always high on the agenda, but the sparse elegance of every piece of design, whether it is a Bang & Olufsen music deck or a Georg Jensen set of cutlery, is a national trademark.

← This old-fashioned car looks quite out of place in the Modernist setting of the Bellavista housing complex on the coast at Klampenborg, just north of Copenhagen. Built in 1935, the bright, white, liner-like design, with its many sea-view balconies, was hailed as a masterpiece, and prompted Jacobsen to be described in the press as "the Danish Corbusier".

↑ Alvar Aalto built his summer house on the island of Muuratsalo, Finland, in 1953. He borrowed from traditional Finnish farm-planning and designed the place around an enclosed courtyard. On the outside of the house he used brick to experiment with texture. Inside it is light-filled, simply furnished, and incorporates an unusual mezzanine level.

← Designed in 1953 by architect Stig Ancker, the Ancker Summer House in Halland, Sweden is a simple L-shaped home. Built with large concrete blocks and painted white, it helped to establish the modern, light, open style that many were to imitate. Inside, the walls, floor, and ceiling are all clad in wood.

designer homes

The homes of architects and designers have long been a test bed for pioneering new ideas. Scandinavian designers are no exception to this, and throughout the last century they have inspired the world in many innovative ways through their informal, elegant, healthy, environmentally thoughtful, and exciting homes and furnishings. Brilliant designers, among them Finn Juhl, Arne Jacobsen, Alvar Aalto, and Bruno Mathsson, produced ideas more than half a century ago that still succeed in feeling fresh and relevant today. Extending the tradition of making living spaces for the modern world, subsequent generations of Scandinavian designers have continued to experiment with ideas in their own homes.

One such pioneer is the Finn designer Antti Nurmesniemi, a household name due to his furniture and product designs. Perhaps his most popular item is the ubiquitous, iconic, brightly coloured, enamelled coffeepots from the late 1950s, but more recently there also have been stripy deckchairs, numerous dining chairs, and even his highly distinctive and beautiful electricity pylons. Less well-known is his waterside home, shown left, where he lives with his wife, the highly respected designer Vuokko Nurmesniemi, who has achieved renown for her textile and clothing designs.

Their home, built in the mid-1970s, is a large rectangular structure on the shore of an island just east of Helsinki. It was a pioneering, hi-tech home when it was first built, with its use of the intriguing steel-web "space construction" structure that is visible at ceiling height. Antti started his working life in a plane factory, where he learned about creating maximum strength with minimum material. This method of construction reduces the need for columns and allows for the creation of larger, open-plan spaces.

The interior is exceptionally open and, unusually, the main living area ranges over three floors. The library and work area cascades down a short flight of stairs into a dining area, and then falls again into an inviting, sunken sitting area. The crossover of industrial design into the home was highly innovative in its time and is typical of Nurmesniemei's approach – the synthesization of the rational and mechanic with organic forms and a human touch. The house features huge windows so it is flooded with natural light, and with the inclusion of a large office area it provides an early example of the dual-role home. It looks fresh and contemporary – just the sort of place that any young, design-aware professional would choose to live in today – which makes it difficult to imagine just how startling it must have looked when it was first built, more than a quarter of a century ago.

← The Nurmesniemi House, 1975, in Helsinki is home to two of Finland's best-known designers Antti and Vuokko Nurmesniemi. Antti is well-known for his furniture and product designs, including the black leather dining chairs, designed in 1960, called Triennial. Vuokko is famous for her textile designs for Marimekko, and she also has her own clothes shop.

→ The home of Danish furniture designer Nanna Ditzel. This large, open-plan space is furnished with light, basketwork furniture and features a typical raised fireplace with adjacent log store.

coastal summer house – helsingborg, sweden

Living close to the sea, lakes, or rivers is one of the dreams of Scandinavian living. Waterside locations are perennial favourites for new homes – vacation homes in particular. Whether in Sweden, Denmark, Norway, or Finland, people share a passion for the water, for bathing, sailing, fishing, or simply looking out over the continually moving and changing landscape.

The Swedish architect Claes von Hauswolff and his family had, for several years, spent their summers and weekends in an old timber cabin close to Helsingborg on the west coast of Sweden, but with the arrival of a fourth child the need for space became a priority. The original cabin contained a sleeping area, a tiny bathroom, a small kitchen, and living space; it measured little more than 25 square metres (269 square feet). "We were already very cosy and even had triple bunks, so we really did need more room," explains von Hauswolff.

The old cabin had been built in the 1950s and stood raised a few centimetres above the ground, on stilts. Von Hauswolff's plan was to dismantle and sell the old building to a friend, who had the idea of moving it across country and relocating it on an island in the archipelago at Stockholm. Such eco-friendly recycling and relocation of old homes is common in Sweden, and is made possible largely by the fact that the structures are timber-built. With little more than a hammer and saw it's possible to deconstruct and reassemble the simply made buildings, loading the panels and sections onto a truck, and driving them to the new location. A new summer house was then to be designed from scratch, taking into account the location, the orientation toward the sun and the views, and protection against the winds.

"It is a really lovely area, very slow and low key and close to a small fishing village of just 100 houses," describes von Hauswolff. "We all love the water, particularly the sea and the beach, but also love to be close to nature. This area is a nature reserve and very rich

↓ The horizontal timber boards and decking have been spaced slightly apart to give a more open and airy feel to the structure. The storage bench was designed by Thomas Sandell for Ikea.

← The generous sunny deck is given welcome shade on hot days by the deep overhang of the roof. From outside on the deck the owners can look across the meadows to the water beyond.

↑ The large, limestone-framed fireplace is shallow but wide to reflect heat back into the room. The furniture is an eclectic mixture of antique and modern pieces.

in birds and other wildlife." The location is the well-known Molle peninsular, which is famous for its beautiful cliffs and for its long reputation as an excellent bathing resort. It grabbed the headlines in the 1920s when it became one of the first places in Sweden where men and women were allowed to bathe in the sea together.

As the design of the new summer house progressed, nostalgia set in. "My wife and children decided that we couldn't possibly sell the old cabin," recalls von Hauswolff. "They felt it was very much a part of their lives and so wanted to keep it." As a result of this, he went back to the drawing board and reworked his designs to incorporate the old cabin with the new design. The result of his efforts is an L-shaped home with the old cabin being used as sleeping quarters, bathroom, and a place for coats and shoes. The new wing, meanwhile, houses the kitchen/dining area and living space. The size of the home has now grown four-fold, from a cramped 25 square metres (269 square feet) to a generous, light, and airy 100 square metres (1,076 square feet).

"The L-shaped design means that the house is secluded from its neighbours and every room has a view of the water." Like the old cabin, this new summer house is raised off the ground. "For us it was important not just to see the sea, but also to see the edge, the moment where the land meets the water," explains von Hauswolff.

The house is built with local Swedish pine, it has a timber frame, and is wrapped around with horizontal pine boards that have been set slightly apart to give the building a more open, spacious feeling. "The carpenter really wasn't very happy about leaving the gaps," says von Hauswolff. "He was worried that it would let in all the spiders and bugs. And he was absolutely right, but we like spiders and bugs, so it is OK." The boarding is used on the whole of the building and also encloses the old cabin. The same, large new windows have been used throughout. The old cabin has been so thoroughly incorporated into the new, it is now virtually impossible to distinguish one from the other.

The kitchen is the hub of the home as the family likes to cook often on weekends and holidays, especially when friends come to stay. A simple, off-the-shelf kitchen system has been installed and given a luxurious edge with the use of a white marble work counter. The unusual, perforated aluminium dining chairs, called Landi, are classics from the late 1930s by Swiss designer Hans Coray. Being lightweight and weatherproof they are ideal for use both inside and out, which means they are perfect for summer house use. The all-white space, including glossy white-painted floor, is especially cool and inviting in the summer.

The living room is a simple, open room with fantastic views. The most striking feature in the room is the fireplace, with its shallow design finished with a pale limestone surround. The living room furniture is a mixture of antique and modern, including contemporary sofas by British designer Jasper Morrison.

Where once families used their holiday houses just in the summertime, there has been a shift in recent years to year-round use. The von Hauswolff family now likes to visit their new summer house as often as possible, throughout the summer and also in the winter months. When the seasons change, the transformation from the bright, open summer house to a cosy, warm winter house is cleverly planned. The lightweight curtains are swapped for heavier ones, thick woollen blankets and cushions in rich, warm colours are strewn around, and, for the finishing touch, the fire is lit.

↑ The all-white kitchen, with its white marble worktops, was designed to reinforce the summery feel of the place. The chairs are 1939 classics by the Swiss designer Hans Coray. Called Landi, the design was revolutionary because it was made using perforated aluminium – a non-corrosive material that makes them ideal for use both inside and out.

colonial style summer house – præstø, denmark

Danish architect Mette Lange has an intense love of India and Indian design. She and her husband, Anders Linnet, and son Jacob spend half of their year living and working in Goa, where Linnet has founded a school project on the banks of the river Tiracol for educating and supporting children of the migrant labour force. The other half of the year is spent in an elegant summer house, which Lange herself has designed, close to the sea, 100km (63 miles) south of Copenhagen. It also overlooks the salt marsh towards the Bøgestrøm strait. As might well be expected, their home is furnished with Indian furniture and artifacts, and has a strong colonial feel.

Lange and Linnet's Danish home is one of a pair – the other was designed for her father and his wife, who visit regularly with Lange's sisters and their young families. By constructing the two simultaneously it was possible to keep building costs to a minimum. "We found the place because my husband's parents had their own summer cottage nearby, and this land came up for sale," recalls Lange. She adds that although it is close to the coast, there is no major sandy beach nearby and so it is much quieter and less populous than the better-known holiday resorts on the same stretch. The sandy areas are easily reached, though, and Lange has a boat moored close to the house for sailing around the coast. Although the two houses were the first ones to be built on this meadow site, at the edge of a salt marsh, planning permission was granted without any major problems as the area is already used extensively for summer homes. The only major restriction was that the buildings should be no more than one storey high.

Both houses are raised on a very large timber-decking platform, which appears to make them almost float above the meadow grasses. They use traditional, inexpensive construction techniques – a pine wood frame raised on foundation piles, which are sunk into the ground – and both have pine cladding and flooring, and are painted in traditional Danish colours – a black-stained exterior and black roof with white windows. However, while they have a traditional feel the designs are also unmistakably modern, and a world away from the family's home in India, which is built in stone on a steep slope in the jungle.

The houses face east, towards the sea, and have one entire floor-to-ceiling wall of windows and sliding doors, which draws in sunlight for most of the day and floods the interiors with natural light. Each of the huge windows is constructed with three large rectangular panes of glass – the shape of the windows emphasizes the long, low horizontal lines of the buildings. To draw extra light into the heart of the house, the roof ridge of each house has a large glass lantern. The eaves of the roof are also very deep and provide shadow and shelter for the deck. Unusually, there is no guttering along the edge of the roof – this was largely for aesthetic reasons in order to make the edge look slender – but rain is kept away from the windows by the generous eaves. When the sliding doors are open onto the deck, the interior and exterior spaces flow together almost magically.

The homes are clearly related in style, but are not identical. Lange's own place is a single, open-plan, rectangular room with a kitchen and dining area at one end. Sofas are placed close to a large, central wood-burning stove, and work tables are positioned near the windows for light. A bed is tucked into the far corner, with the doorway to the small bathroom and nursery behind it. The second house has a single cooking-dining-living room.

← Much of the furniture in architect Mette Lange's home was imported from Kerala in southern India. The twin columns, in hard cherry wood, arrived in the same consignment. They have been lengthened with the addition of stainless steel bases, which make an interesting contrast to the wood. The contemporary-style wood burning stove takes pride of place.

↓ Two houses, designed as a pair by Mette Lange, sit side by side and are surrounded by a timber deck, which makes them appear to float over the meadow. They are finished in traditional colours – black wood with white windows.

The two bedrooms are set slightly apart from the main living space and are reached by walking through an outdoor passage. The breeze channelled through the passage cools the bedrooms on warm summer evenings.

Inside, Lange's home has a powerful colonial feel and is furnished largely with items imported from India. "My husband used to run a café in Copenhagen and then had an idea about setting up a shop selling colonial-style furniture. He bought the entire contents of a Keralan house, shipped it in a container to Denmark, and stored everything in the café cellar. The shop idea didn't ever happen and so when we came to work on this house, we looked into the cellar and dusted off all this treasure." Along with the beautiful hardwood furniture, the home also incorporates two very distinctive rose wood columns, which, for extra height, stand on stainless steel feet. "The steel provides an interesting contrast to the beautiful old wood," comments Lange. Further Indian columns are used outside to support the roof, which covers a dining area.

The same rich hardwood is to be found in the panels that run along the inside of the entire back wall of the space, and on the front of the island counter in the kitchen, which faces the dining table. Again, here the wood is used to contrast with the contemporary style stainless steel kitchen. Suspended over this counter is an intriguing hanging rail – at first it looks as though it may have come with the Indian consignment, but on closer inspection it is the slender trunk of a silver birch tree that was found locally.

The one very obvious Danish feature of the interior is the modern, cast-iron, wood-burning stove, which takes a central position between the dining area and the rest of the space. The galleon suspended in the glass roof lantern is also Danish, and made by craftsmen working locally to the summer houses.

↓ (left) A large, glass roof lantern provides the perfect place for floating this handsome model galleon. The roof light also allows sunlight to penetrate right into the heart of the building.

↓ (right) The open-plan kitchen basks in sunlight, casting the shadow of the hanging galleon onto the side of the Indian cherry wood-clad island unit. The unusual hanging rail is a slender, silver birch tree-trunk that was found in the garden.

→ The interior, with its stylish Indian furniture, has a cool and spacious Colonial feel to it. Even the buffalo head on the wall above the door was included in the consignment of furniture from southern India.

↓ (Overleaf) Both summer houses seen at dusk, illuminated from the inside. The deep eaves provide shelter over the deck, and the glass lanterns stand above the roof ridge.

→ The stepped levels of the timber decking fit over the rocky, boulder-strewn landscape. A generous canopy, projecting out over the deck, provides a sheltered place for sitting outside.

↑ A pair of plump, pale yellow sofas make a comfortable, sunny seating area in the heart of the living space. Floor-to-ceiling windows and doors let light flood in and provide sea views.

maritime home – stockholm archipelago, sweden

The rocky, boulder-strewn banks of a remote island in the vast Stockholm archipelago was spotted by a passing yachtsman as the dream site for a summer house. He bought the site and commissioned Landström Arkitekter to design a home with a nautical feel.

The completed project includes a main house, a guest house, and a sauna. Each is fitted sensitively into the landscape and ideally positioned to enjoy the amazing views. "We have interpreted the idea of a marine character through the use of a system of wires and rigging screws, similar to the rigging of a mast," explains Jochen Werner of Landström. "On the inside of the house, steel tension cables can be seen stretching above the living space. They connect the roof with the central floor structure and tie the whole together." The sauna continues the maritime theme. "It acts like a look-out or captain's bridge and has a spectacular view over the archipelago bay."

The pine-built house rises up from a series of gently stepped wooden terraces, which change level in order to fit over the rockbed. The entrance is tucked under a deep sheltering canopy, and the distinctive windows are of a Swedish design that has been developed to withstand the harshest of weather – they are built using core timber, the wood closest to the heart of a trunk, which is harder and more durable than the softer outer layers of wood. Core timber is also used in the roof construction, and the detailing has been completed in zinc. The house exterior is clad in horizontal timber boarding – the subtle horizontal lines give the house the appearance of hunkering down into the landscape. This boarding is painted with a solution of ferrous sulphate, which helps to protect the wood panelling from the harsh weather that blows across the archipelago.

Because of the environmentally sensitive nature of the archipelago, planning restrictions are strict and numerous. New homes usually can be built only if they are

↑ The maritime theme of this house is evident in the use of steel tension cables, which act as a brace for the structure, and the white painted, wooden boarding that lines the interior. The cherry wood kitchen can be seen in the distance.

actually replacing an older structure. Permission was granted in this case as the new house was replacing a smaller 1930s summer house, which had been located on the same spot. While the remote location clearly had enormous appeal in terms of enjoying the landscape, it did, however, provide a serious challenge to the builders. All the materials and workers for this project had to be delivered by boat, and it took several journeys to transport them all. "Everything had to be delivered in small pieces and then constructed on site, for example it was impossible to deliver ready-made large panels for the building because they just wouldn't fit on the boat," explains Werner. The island is at least an hour's sailing time from Stockholm, so it made sense for the building team to actually live on the island itself during the six-month construction process.

Inside, the space at ground level is open-plan, with a long dining table close to the seaward windows and a soft seating area, with sunny yellow sofas, behind it. The kitchen is incorporated into the open-plan space and is fitted with units in a warm cherry wood finish. All the rooms are lined with white-painted, vertical timber boarding and, once again, the board has been used in a subtle way – by fixing the boards vertically, it has emphasized the height of the rooms. Although the house is primarily intended to be used in the summer, a large, central fireplace has been built, as the owner does also like to visit, when possible, during the winter and spring months. The bedrooms are accommodated on an upper floor, which sits in the middle of the home and makes it possible for parts of the perimeter of the ground floor, including the dining area, to have an exciting double height space. It is here that it is possible to see the steel tension cables running between the roof and floor. Meanwhile, the seating area sits under the lower, bedroom level and has a more relaxed, tranquil feel to it. Furniture throughout the house is mostly simple, contemporary, and comfortable. Soft touches are added with big, colourful, abstract-patterned rugs.

↓ The house has been designed to withstand the harsh winter weather that is typical of this waterside location. The large window frames were built using the particularly hard and durable timber found close to the trunk core.

↑ This 70-year-old, cliff-top summer house, in Jutland, Denmark, has been completely renovated by its owners. To create a startling contrast, they have painted the exterior black and the interior white. Natural linen has been used extensively in the furnishings, including these soft window blinds.

scandinavian tradition

Even the smallest of Scandinavian summer houses are loved and treasured by their owners. Many have been handed down through generations, with each making their own changes and new additions. Furnishings are very often an intriguing blend of items that have been collected together over the decades and are likely to be highly functional – chairs that can be simply painted to smarten them up when they get tatty, and sofas with removable, washable covers. After all, the summer house is not a place where you want to spend time on household chores and DIY, it is all about being outside and enjoying nature.

Older summer house designs were considerably smaller than those being built today, and it is still not unusual to find entire families staying in older houses that have a floor area of little more than 25–30 square metres (270–320 square feet). Many of these buildings are no more than beach huts, with a sleeping room and a living room with a rudimentary sink and stove. The older designs also tend to be fairly basic in terms of services and comfort, and have small windows, which tends to make them dark inside. However, most Scandinavians will agree that any sort of summer house is better than none at all.

Before the tradition of summer houses became so firmly established, it was usual in the early 20th century for poor fishing families to supplement their incomes by letting all or part of their houses to city dwellers who wanted to spend their summer close to the sea and in the fresh air. Gradually, in many areas, the fishing villages became transformed into resorts, and city families began to buy up and take over the traditional homes. One typical example of this is at Tisvildeleje in Denmark, where today most of the houses are summer houses for Copenhageners.

↑ (left) This beautiful, 100-year-old fisherman's house is designed in a simple and yet romantic style. It is located in the hamlet of Tisvildeleje, in the northern part of the Danish island of Zealand, which has, for generations, been a favourite summer holiday retreat for the people of Copenhagen.

↑ (right) This summery courtyard makes a lovely sheltered and enclosed dining area. The black exterior of the house, shown opposite, can be seen to the side of the picture.

oak-built cabin – vestfold, norway

In many cases building homes close to the water presents problems, either because of the difficult rocky terrain or the sensitive nature of the landscape. In this case, the major problem, according to architect Einar Jarmund of Jarmund/Vigsnæs, was that the area it was being built in was so beautiful. "The challenge was to make a house that could sit comfortably and hold its own in the space between a wonderful oak forest and the water line." Jarmund's response was to create a long, low cabin with a zinc roof, built using oak – an expensive, luxury material chosen to relate to the oak forest behind. The house is meant as a marker, to act as a pause between the forest and the sea. Another additional challenge that he came up against was to take into account the geographical contradiction of the site – the views across the water were to the north, while the sun came from the south. This was overcome by planning the interior to follow the path of the sun from east to west. Bedrooms were positioned to receive sunlight in the morning and the living space to get the afternoon and evening sun.

Inside, the entire space is lined with Norwegian and Swedish oak, which has been whitewashed to emphasize the pattern of the grain. Large banks of windows and an outside dining terrace ensure that the views can be fully enjoyed. "It is the perfect site for summer holidays," says Jarmund. "Summer is what we live for. In Norway we have the same amount of sun as everyone else, it just happens that we have most of it during the summer, so a house is the staging of a summer dream and must be designed to make the most of it." The unusual, outward-leaning exterior walls are a visual reference to the well-known Norwegian seaside ice cream kiosks that used to be made close to this site. Just like the the cabin, the kiosks also had zinc roofs.

↓ (left) This contemporary, Norwegian summer house lies just a few metres from the water. The low lines and wood cladding are reminiscent of marine buildings such as boat sheds.

↓ (right) The fantastic, gnarled old tree and the new canopy frame the view from the dining terrace.

→ Nature is always present in this Norwegian house. The windows in the bedroom are set in the outward-sloping wall and open onto a clearing, which is dotted with silver birch trees.

← Built on the site of a ferry landing-stage and an old hotel, this contemporary Danish home, by architect Poul Frær Hansen, is situated in a stunning waterside location. The vast, floor-to-ceiling windows in the towering dining room make the most of the beautiful views. A teak dining table takes centrestage, with Philippe Starck designed chairs, and a contemporary chandelier by Italian manufacturer Flos.

water and sky

The two most powerful natural elements in any coastal region are water and sky, and both of these elements have provided inspiration for architects and designers.

Together with taking ideas from the architecture of ships, designers have also been inspired by coastal buildings, the ancient homes of fishing families, boat sheds, net stores, waterside warehouses, and ferry landings. The way that these buildings fit the landscape, cantilever over the water, or are simply designed to serve their purpose has an appeal to architects, who like to emphasize rational and functional design. These old marine buildings, almost always built in timber, have been readily converted into other uses too. A charming and much-photographed example of this is the old boat house at Louisiana, on the coast just north of Copenhagen in Denmark. This place is the location of the famous Louisiana Museum of Modern Art and gallery, founded by Knud Jensen in the late 1950s. The old boat house became a guest house and studio for visiting artists, and was eventually converted again into an office and sitting room for Jensen. It is still furnished with the distinctive Poul Kjærholm chairs, stools, and tables, which were used in the gallery's interior in the early years. Every day Jensen would walk through the museum towards his office and, in true romantic Scandinavian fashion, was known to relish the moment he entered his shoreline office, with its huge windows, so that he could enjoy the sea views.

New and remodelled waterside homes often take the water as the focus of their design. For example, main windows and outdoor terraces are usually orientated to take advantage of the outlook, with windows being made as large as possible to enjoy the views, and to take in the wide-open Scandinavian skies. In many cases, waterside homes are built on stilts, partly for the views but also for practical reasons – to avoid the danger of flooding

↑ Founder of the world-famous, shore-line Louisiana Museum of Modern Art, the late Knud Jensen converted an old boat house to make this office and studio. It is furnished with Danish classics: in the foreground are chairs, stools, and loungers by Poul Kjærholm; on the left is the distinctive Egg chair by Arne Jacobsen; and at the back, dining chairs by Hans Wegner sit under a PH Artichoke lamp by Poul Henningsen.

↑ (left) Neat geometry underpins the design of this bathroom. The grid of square window panes is echoed in the square wall and floor tiles. Offset against this are the horizontal lines of the sink counter, wall cupboard, and shelf.

↑ (right) The weather on the Norwegian coast can be rough, so this enclosed courtyard provides a wonderful suntrap with protection from winds blowing off the sea. The owners asked architect Odd Magne Vatne to design a contemporary interpretation of a Functionalist style house.

→ Situated on the western coast of Norway, close to Stavanger, this house is set low into the landscape, but still manages to take advantage of the stunning views. One entire wall of the living room is a window onto the sea.

and to minimize the impact of the structure on the environment. The skill of the best designs is in the blurring of the boundaries between land and sea. This may include such delights as capturing the reflections of rippling water on walls and ceilings, and there is often a crossover of materials – sail canvas used as a sun shade, or thick rope for a stair handrail.

Numerous designers have also taken their inspiration from the water for furniture and products. Perhaps the most famous has to be Alvar Aalto's 1930s vase, designed for the Savoy in Helsinki – its irregular shape is reputed to have been derived from the wavy shorelines of Finnish lakes. Even the glass itself has an animated, watery quality. Its intriguing, fluid appearance is made possible by the fact that the pieces are hand-blown into a wooden mould, a process that gives the glass vase its trademark rippled walls. Along with the numerous versions of this famous vase, Aalto reused the coastline shape for other glass designs, including a range of serving dishes in his Eskimoerindens skinnbuxa series. (Interestingly the word Aalto is Finnish for wave.) The influence of water and its organic flowing lines can be found in dozens of Aalto's designs – serpentine, curved plywood frames for chairs and loungers, as well as his curvy, freestanding screens. These organic forms can be found in the work of numerous other Scandinavian designers too, and the appealing softness is partly what marks out Scandinavian Modernism from the harder-edged style of Modernism found elsewhere.

To this day, the inspiration of water is omnipresent: Finnish design company Snowcrash recently created eye-catching "Soundwave" sound-proofing panels, which are formed in the shape of a seascape, and Swedish designer Lena Bergström has designed beautiful glass candle holders that are made in the shape of softly rounded pebbles.

↑ Set across the water from Oslo, this home, designed by Jarmund/Vigsnæs, is wrapped in windows, providing a 180 degree outlook. The kitchen is a Bulthaup system, and the Danish owners have introduced the classic Arne Jacobsen-designed Series 7 dining chairs.

a house with bay views – near oslo, norway

One of the great things about waterside living in Scandinavian countries, especially when close to the big cities, is the network of efficient water transport. The ferries and water taxis have opened up the possibilities of living within easy commuting distance of cities, and yet being able still to enjoy a fantastic waterside setting.

Taking the ferry to work in Oslo across the stunning wide bay has become a daily reality for the owners of this new home. The building is perched on a steep, rocky site that is studded with small fir trees. "To make the most of the view, we lifted the building up above the trees and placed the living areas on the upper level, with sleeping accommodation downstairs," explains architect Håkon Vigsnæs of Jarmund/Vigsnæs. "We were also concerned not to interfere too much with the natural landscape. It might have been expected to blast the boulders out of the way to make a level base for the house, but instead we brought concrete onto the site and cast it in place to fit round the rocks."

A timber frame structure was constructed for the living level, which has a band of windows that face northward towards Oslo. "The house stretches out to make the most of the sun and to take in the 180 degree views of the city and its surroundings." The building is an L shape and the large terrace sits over the bedrooms below – it is reached through the light and open kitchen and dining area. The airy lightness of the kitchen space is emphasized by the floor-to-ceiling windows and doors, the white Bulthaup kitchen, and the white dining table with its Arne Jacobsen-designed Series 7 chairs. The living room is furnished in softer colours and has a cosy, central fireplace. It is given an altogether different, more restful character from the kitchen area by the subtle addition of a deeper band of horizontal boarding at roof level. The exterior wood is untreated larch, which will weather in time to a soft silver-grey colour.

↓ The terrace in this house sits on top of the ground floor bedrooms and is finished with steel balustrading and canvas panels. The entire upper floor is given over to living space, with the kitchen and dining area located to the left, and the living area to the right.

→ The deep timber deck makes a perfect dining area with impressive views. Untreated larch wood was chosen as a cladding because it can cope with wide changes in humidity, and will eventually weather to a soft, silver-grey finish.

↑ Even in the city, Scandinavians love to be close to nature. This exciting, new waterside development, called Gashaga Brygga, is by rising Swedish stars Sandell Sandberg. The jetty stretches out over the water and the exterior finishes include sandblasted stainless steel panels and larch wood.

→ The interiors feature dramatic double-height spaces. The loft living that has become so popular in the USA and the UK has not yet become a major feature of Scandinavian urban design, but the generous sense of space and light here has made these highly desirable homes.

↑ The dining area is lined entirely with timber boarding – the walls are painted white and the floor a soft grey. The window at the end of the table could almost be mistaken for a picture as it frames the view outside. The distinctively shaped dining chairs are part of the Latta series by the designer of the house, Anna von Schewen.

family home – stockholm archipelago, sweden

When designer Anna von Schewen was asked by her brother to create a new family home, her approach was to work from the inside out. "I wanted to focus on the basics and look at the way the house would be used. It naturally divided into three zones – a place for sleeping, a place for cooking, and a living-dining room for sharing meals with friends, and enjoying the views and nature," says von Schewen, an interior architect and furniture designer.

The house design reflects and builds on von Schewen's approach to designing furniture, where she starts with the body and looks for ways of making the furniture, particularly chairs, fit the body's contours. Her ultimate goal is to create a design that follows the lines of the body and fits it in much the same way that clothes do. She is particularly well-known for her Latta chair, built with strips of sensuously curved and pliable laminated wood and covered with a woven fabric. The flexibility of these materials means that when the chair is sat on, the whole unit bends and moulds itself into the shape of the body. Included in the Latta series is the intriguing Latta wall – conceived for use in the dark Swedish winters. It is a semi-transparent wall constructed of fabric that has been stretched across light tubes, which glow brightly in the mornings. The idea is that, by imitating natural sunlight, the light is bright enough to wake you up, and so replaces the jarring effect of an alarm clock. Von Schewen applied this people-centred approach to her ideas for this new house, as it was designed specifically to fit her family and its needs.

The house was eventually located in the Stockholm archipelago, around 80km (50 miles) north of the Swedish capital. As is often the case with new waterside homes in Scandinavia, the house replaced an older building that had previously occupied the site. The existing summer cabin dated from the 1940s, and, typical of its period, was a modest size at just 25 square metres (269 square feet).

The concept of dividing the home into three areas is expressed in the design, as the house was formed from three individual but linked "boxes". The journey through the spaces follows a progression from the very public family and entertaining space in the living room, to the semi-private kitchen area, and then the more private sleeping and bathing quarters. While the design is contemporary in style the construction is traditional, and is based on a timber frame with timber cladding. Pine is used as the main material, and, in common with many Swedish holiday homes, the exterior is stained black. Interestingly, though, patches of colour have also been introduced, such as the blue stain on the doors. "Although we used traditional materials, there were some discussions with the planning authorities about the design of the house," recalls von Schewen. "At first there were questions about the roof shape for the living area." The single sloping roof rises up to the chimney, which is at the heart of the home. "The problem was that it isn't a regular pitched roof, but eventually the planners were persuaded that it was OK."

Directly beneath the roof is the main living and dining room, which has just one solid wall to the outside and is faced entirely in glass on the other two sides. The glass walls are divided into three huge vertical panels and the transparency of the space gives the family the close contact it wanted with the surrounding landscape. The house has water on both sides and the large expanses of glass give the room the impression almost of being open,

↑ With its parallel, all-glass walls, this Swedish summer house almost melts into the landscape. The huge expanses of glass on both sides of the building not only offer great views from inside, but they also make it possible to see right through the house to the view on the other side. The large, oval floor lamp behind the plant pot is another of Anna von Schewen's designs.

like an open pavilion in the garden, as the views can be seen right the way through the house. From the outside, the windows also provide intriguing reflections of the surrounding trees. Inside, the white-painted and timber-lined room is light and spacious, and at certain times of day the sloping ceiling picks up animated reflections from the nearby water. "It is very restful to watch the evening sun bouncing off the water and reflecting its patterns and colours on the ceiling," describes von Schewen.

Next to the open living and dining area is the kitchen – the hub of the home and a space that is more enclosed than the living room. This room also has large windows but this time they are horizontal, giving the same magnificent views, but at the same time managing to retain a cosy feeling in the room. The kitchen is lined with neat rows of fitted storage cupboards that are kept below the work counter level in order to maintain a sense of space and airiness in the room. Storage above the cupboards is provided by open shelving. Another practical and decorative storage feature is the large recess in the kitchen specifically for storing logs. While this is a weekend and holiday home, the family does not restrict it to summer use only as they like to escape from the city all year round. So the major, and vital, feature of the home is the large central fireplace – there is an open fire in the living room, on the back of which is a stove for the kitchen.

In general the interior is kept as simple as possible, and is lined with vertical timber boarding, which has been painted white. The furniture is contemporary in style and includes some of von Schewen's well-known designs, including the Latta chairs and a Latta lamp – a large egg-shaped floor lamp. The colour scheme is predominantly white, with bold splashes of colour introduced in the furnishings, particularly the striped rugs.

↑ The neutral backdrop of this living room is given a splash of zesty colour with the addition of the striped rug. The wire chair is a classic by Harry Bertoia, while the dining chairs and the unusual low-level chair are from the Latta series by Anna von Schewen.

house and annexe – stockholm archipelago, sweden

The Stockholm archipelago consists of more than 24,000 islands set in a vast expanse of sea. It is located to the east and north-east of Stockholm, where Lake Malaren enters the Baltic Sea. Up until the late 19th century it was home to remote farming, fishing, and hunting communities, but it was with the invention of the steamship that this amazing, natural playground began to open up to more visitors.

Artists and writers were among the first to discover the beauty and peace of this area – the Swedish playwright August Strindberg described his first impressions in a fictionalized autobiography, *The Son of a Servant*: "rough granite islets with pine forests … stormy bay waters … not the Alps of Switzerland, nor the olive hills of the Mediterranean, or the chalk cliffs of Normandy could ever force aside this rival". However, at the turn of the 20th century the archipelago soon became hugely popular with families, particularly the

↓ The raised terrace on this Swedish waterside home is reminiscent of the crow's nest on a boat. It provides a sheltered space to enjoy the sun and the views over the tree-tops.

↑ An idyllic boat house with floating pontoon is the perfect spot for messing about on the water. The suspended fisherman's lamp completes the picture.

wealthier merchant classes, who began to commission the building of idyllic summer houses. It was to these retreats that families would escape the city during the summer and enjoy the healthy pursuits of the sea and countryside. Due to the proximity of many of the islands to Stockholm, often husbands would continue to commute to work in the city.

Today, holidaymakers still come here to take it easy, sail, swim, and soak up the sun. The water is criss-crossed with ferries, making even the most far-flung islands accessible. Of the many islands, some are large and others small, some remain uninhabited, and some are privately owned with just enough room for a small summer house and boat mooring. The larger islands have become favourite holiday spots, with hotels, youth hostels, and some of Sweden's finest restaurants found on them. Many of the islands are also classified as nature reserves, which means that, despite its popularity, the archipelago has managed to retain its natural charm, and remain rich in wildlife.

Continuing a long tradition of summer-house building in the Stockholm archipelago, this striking, contemporary, two-storey home has taken its inspiration from maritime architecture. "Just like a boat, it has the living space on the upper level with an open deck looking out to the water, and you go downstairs for the sleeping quarters," describes architect Anders Landström of Landström Arkitekter.

The house was commissioned by a couple with one child. Based in Stockholm, they loved to mess around with boats and wanted a weekend and holiday retreat that was within easy reach of the city. The site that was eventually chosen is within a one-hour motorboat ride from Stockholm and sits up above the water line, offering excellent views of the extraordinary waterscape. "The path of the sun, as it moves across the sky during the course of the day, is very important in the design of the house," explains Landström. "The deck is designed at one side of the house because that is where the morning sun falls, making it a perfect place for breakfast. However, it is equally good in the evening because from here it is possible to watch the sun set over the trees."

Inside, the upper floor comprises a large living space with a small kitchen. "Just as you'd find on a boat, this is a small, handcrafted space lined with units." In keeping with kitchens found on boats, there are finger holes for opening the cupboard doors and drawers instead of handles, so that you don't knock into them in the small space. For a splash of intense colour, the ceiling is painted cobalt blue. The bedrooms are situated on the ground level and are designed in the style of fitted ship cabins.

In addition to the house, the architect also designed an exciting annexe situated much closer to the water's edge. The annexe houses two guest suites, a sauna, and a large store for boats and canoes. The heart of the space is taken up with a covered deck, perfect for sitting out on balmy summer evenings, which leads to a floating pontoon.

↓ While conventional in shape, this house in the Swedish archipelago is unmistakably contemporary in style. The inside arrangement is upside down, with sleeping and bathing areas at ground level and a light and spacious living area above leading onto the asymmetrical sun deck.

→ The kitchen, built in cherry wood and featuring flush-finish doors and drawers, is compact but elegant. The eye is drawn through the space and into the landscape beyond. Colour is added with the rich blue ceiling.

baltic summer house – fårö, sweden

As the summers are fairly short in Scandinavian countries, the beach becomes the focus of attention as soon as the sun starts to shine. The change of season and the arrival of spring is marked with huge bonfires at the end of April. But this festival is small compared to the revelries of midsummer, in late June, when, particularly in Norway, Sweden, and Denmark, chains of bonfires are lit along huge stretches of coast, and there is midsummer pole dancing and singing. In Sweden the festival is marked with a traditional lunch of herring and boiled new potatoes, which is eaten outdoors regardless of the weather.

The Baltic seaside summer house shown on these pages belongs to, and was designed by, Swedish architect Gunnar Tarras Hollström. Like many summer cabins it has grown over the years. "We began in 1954 with a very simple, very small place of no more than 20 square metres," he recalls. "Over the years we have added an extra room here and there, and an upper floor". The oldest section of the building is at the back, and contains a kitchen, bedroom, and bathroom. In 1960 a side extension was added for a bedroom suite, in the 1970s came a separate guest annexe, and then, in the 1990s, the top floor, with a small outside balcony, and a downstairs dining area.

The summer house is built traditionally, using Swedish pine, and the entire structure sits on foundations sunk into the sand. "Of course it would be completely impossible to build like this today, there are very tough restrictions that make it impossible to put any new structure within at least 300 metres of the water's edge. But we are just 100 metres from the sea," says Hollström. Following Swedish tradition, the exterior is painted black, with detailing, such as windows and doors, picked out in white. The inside is painted white and furnished with an eclectic and homely mixture of furniture, some items dating back to 1954 and some, such as the trolley on wheels, designed in the intervening years by Hollström.

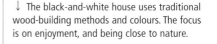

↓ The black-and-white house uses traditional wood-building methods and colours. The focus is on enjoyment, and being close to nature.

← When the Swedish sun shines on this simple, white-painted interior it becomes a perfect beach house – and it could hardly be closer to the sea. Designed by architect Gunnar Tarras Hollström, this large, two-storey, wood-built structure actually sits right on the sand.

→ This covered terrace leads directly out from the dining area. The simple geometry of the design as a whole, and of the built-in bench, is reminiscent of Japanese architecture.

↑ This waterside home, by Norwegian architect Birger Lambertz-Nilsen, was designed to respond to its dramatic, craggy setting. A small jetty is cantilvered from the bottom of the rock, which is ideal for mooring boats and for diving into the cool waters.

house on the rocks – southern coast of norway

This dramatic, craggy setting makes the perfect spot for a summer hideaway. The holiday home of architect Birger Lambertz-Nilsen has fantastic views across a series of islands and the seas that wash the southern coast of Norway. By the waterline there is a simple jetty for mooring boats, and for diving into the refreshing, chilly waters.

"We began the building in the 1960s with the idea of making a house that fitted into the site between the rocks and trees," explains Lambertz-Nilsen, adding that in the ensuing decades extensions have gradually expanded the place. Built using local pine, "the wood has been left completely in its natural state and allowed to weather and turn a silvery grey to match the rocks." The only other material used in the construction is brick, which is made into a powerful double fireplace and chimney that rises through the centre of the house. "Many people have said that the house has a Japanese character, and while I do admire Japanese design it wasn't a conscious decision to follow that style. It is more the case that the philosophy of using materials in an economic and simple way has produced a look that people associate with Japanese design."

Most of the furniture in the house has been built-in. Another attractive detail is the inside-outside terrace, which leads from the dining area. It is roofed over in order to protect it from the weather, and has an open balcony, which frames the stunning views beyond. The bedrooms are simple cabins with built-in storage and long, horizontal windows. There are also two workrooms, one for Lambertz-Nilsen's wife, who is a weaver, and a small drafting office for Lambert-Nilsen himself.

← The warm and welcoming interior is lined with natural pine and features a monumental, brick-built, raised-level fireplace. The unusual corner windows make the most of the views.

↑ The bedrooms are like ships' cabins: furniture is built-in, and long windows frame the stunning views. The horizontal line of the windows emphasizes the tranquillity of the place.

← Owner and architect Birger Lambertz-Nilsen has situated his design studio at the top of the house. His desk is positioned in front of the window, which has an unusual grid-like frame.

the ultimate batchelor pad – espoo, finland

Arriving at this house in the Finnish countryside, visitors are greeted by a blank white wall – the house has turned its back against the cold north, giving few clues about what to expect inside. However, the drama begins when you cross the bridge toward the tall, narrow entrance, and start to get a glimpse of what lies beyond. Inside the entrance hall the house suddenly bursts open into a fan shape, which faces west towards a spectacular landscape and the distant sea beyond. In contrast with the blank exterior wall, this side of the house is open, and finished with huge areas of glass. It sits under a great swooping roof, with undulating eaves built in wood, wrapped in steel, and supported by long, inclined steel columns that are rooted in the rock far below, effectively anchoring the house to its site.

The interior is divided into two wings – one wing contains a swimming pool and sauna and leads onto a large open terrace on one side, while the two, modest-sized bedrooms sit in the second wing, opposite. Up the dramatic, swooping steel and plywood stairway, described as the "dancing staircase" by architect Jyrki Tasa, is the huge living room to one side and a cosy kitchen and dining area on the other. A chimney rises through the house and opens into fireplaces in the swimming pool and living room. The house was designed as the ultimate bachelor pad for entertaining – "the living areas are as large as possible, and are designed as places to enjoy the space and the views," explains Tasa. "By contrast, the bedrooms are much less important and are deliberately kept small."

The house is built from typically Finnish materials. Plywood is a major feature – pine-faced ply wraps round the staircase, is used to make the stair treads themselves, and is also used in large panels to line the walls. The plywood has been used in a contemporary way, and is given an appealing edginess by being combined with steel, glass, and concrete.

↓ The building, designed by Finnish architect Jyrki Tasa, resembles an exotic bird that has landed in the landscape. It is composed of a collection of blocks – the large glass area to the left contains the living room with swimming pool below, while the more enclosed space to the right contains the kitchen and dining room.

→ This intriguing contemporary Finnish home was designed as the ultimate bachelor pad. It is set high on a rock with sea views, and has generous living and entertaining space. Materials include steel and plywood panels.

urban

building utopia

In the years before the end of the 19th century, as Scandinavian countries were in a whirl of change, the main cities grew at an astonishing rate. A decline in farming drove rural people off the land and towards urban areas in search of jobs in the new factories. For the rich, life was good. Their businesses prospered and they lived comfortably in newly built apartments, with all the benefits of the modern age, including electricity, an expanding rail network, and the telephone. (In 1885 Stockholm had more telephones than any other city in the world.) However, for millions of ordinary people life in the city was tough, with overcrowding and frequent outbreaks of disease. Many had simply swapped one set of wretched conditions for another. By 1900 Stockholm had 300,000 inhabitants, one quarter of them living as families in a single room with a kitchen, and the population of Helsinki trebled between 1890 and 1914. One way out was to emigrate; between 1868 and 1872 125,000 Swedes left, mostly for North America.

The growing disparity between rich and poor worried politicians, social reformers, artists, and architects. The harsh conditions fuelled public unrest, causing a general strike in Finland in 1905, and food riots in Sweden in 1917. To diffuse this potential time bomb, societies, groups, and commissions were formed to create visions of an improved world. From these, an ideal emerged for a society where economic and social barriers were broken down, where fairness prevailed, and where the poor and badly educated received welfare to help improve their lives. Housing was at the centre of this debate – it was agreed that the health of the nation was built on the health of the family, which meant that comfortable, hygienic, well-furnished homes were essential.

There then followed decades of large housing exhibitions, including the Stockholm Exhibition of 1909, the 1914 Baltic Exhibition at Malmo, the record-breaking 1929 Architects' Building and Housing Exhibition in Copenhagen, and the great Stockholm Exhibition of 1930. Many had huge ambitions, and included the display of whole houses as well as interior sets to give visitors a glimpse of the new world to come. The 1930 Stockholm show was reviewed for the Finnish architecture press by Alvar Aalto – "The exhibition speaks out for joyful and spontaneous everyday life. And consistently propagates a healthy and unpretentious lifestyle based on economic realities". There was huge public appetite for these events – the 1930 Stockholm show, for example, attracted a staggering four million people to see the radical, functionalist

← Helsinki at the turn of the century looked much like any other city in Europe. However, growing disparity between the rich and the poor was starting to concern politicians and social reformers.

→ The long upper landing at the Snellman house, designed by the Swedish architect Eric Gunnar Asplund and built on the outskirts of Stockholm in 1917. The stripped-back, Neo-classical style marked the bridge between the heavy interiors of the 19th century and the clear, modern designs that were to come from the 1930s onwards.

building utopia

In the years before the end of the 19th century, as Scandinavian countries were in a whirl of change, the main cities grew at an astonishing rate. A decline in farming drove rural people off the land and towards urban areas in search of jobs in the new factories. For the rich, life was good. Their businesses prospered and they lived comfortably in newly built apartments, with all the benefits of the modern age, including electricity, an expanding rail network, and the telephone. (In 1885 Stockholm had more telephones than any other city in the world.) However, for millions of ordinary people life in the city was tough, with overcrowding and frequent outbreaks of disease. Many had simply swapped one set of wretched conditions for another. By 1900 Stockholm had 300,000 inhabitants, one quarter of them living as families in a single room with a kitchen, and the population of Helsinki trebled between 1890 and 1914. One way out was to emigrate; between 1868 and 1872 125,000 Swedes left, mostly for North America.

The growing disparity between rich and poor worried politicians, social reformers, artists, and architects. The harsh conditions fuelled public unrest, causing a general strike in Finland in 1905, and food riots in Sweden in 1917. To diffuse this potential time bomb, societies, groups, and commissions were formed to create visions of an improved world. From these, an ideal emerged for a society where economic and social barriers were broken down, where fairness prevailed, and where the poor and badly educated received welfare to help improve their lives. Housing was at the centre of this debate – it was agreed that the health of the nation was built on the health of the family, which meant that comfortable, hygienic, well-furnished homes were essential.

There then followed decades of large housing exhibitions, including the Stockholm Exhibition of 1909, the 1914 Baltic Exhibition at Malmo, the record-breaking 1929 Architects' Building and Housing Exhibition in Copenhagen, and the great Stockholm Exhibition of 1930. Many had huge ambitions, and included the display of whole houses as well as interior sets to give visitors a glimpse of the new world to come. The 1930 Stockholm show was reviewed for the Finnish architecture press by Alvar Aalto – "The exhibition speaks out for joyful and spontaneous everyday life. And consistently propagates a healthy and unpretentious lifestyle based on economic realities". There was huge public appetite for these events – the 1930 Stockholm show, for example, attracted a staggering four million people to see the radical, functionalist

← The Ränangen House, Djursholm, near Stockholm, Sweden was designed in 1951 by Leonie and Charles-Edouard Geisendorf. This seminal home helped to crystalize what became known as Scandinavian Style. It has a simple and restful, open-plan interior with a large, natural brick wall, an off-centre fireplace, curved ceiling, big windows, and a plain wood floor.

→ In the early 1960s, the arrival of television created interesting design challenges in planning rooms to accommodate it. This interior was shot for the Danish interior design magazine *Bo Bedre* in the early '60s, and at the time around 36 per cent of the Danish population had a television set.

enduring style – finn juhl

One of the hugely appealing qualities of the Scandinavian Modern style is its timelessness. Many of the homes, even those built as early as the 1940s, still manage to retain a certain freshness to this day. The home of Danish designer Finn Juhl is one example of this. Based in a suburb of Copenhagen, this modest single-storey home, with 170 square metres (1,830 square feet) of floorspace, is as comfortable and functional as it was when he designed it in 1942. The only clues to its period are the small bathrooms and galley kitchen, which today would be given more room. The open-plan living spaces, with floor-to-ceiling windows and doors, the large airy bedrooms, and the home office are the sort of spaces that we have come to expect in contemporary homes. Other extraordinary features are that it continues to be lived in by Finn Juhl's partner, Hanne Wilhelm Hansen, and that it still contains almost all the original furniture, built-in fittings, rugs, lighting, ceramics, and even wooden bowls that Juhl designed for the place.

Finn Juhl (1912–1989) was one of a generation of Scandinavian architects inspired by the great 1930 Stockholm Exhibition. The startling, fresh style of the new glass and steel architecture lit his imagination and inspired him, only months later, to enrol as an architecture student. His working life began in the office of leading architect Vilhelm Lauritzen, with whom he worked on such high-profile projects as Copenhagen Airport and the head office and concert hall of the Danish Broadcasting Corporation. Immediately after World War II he set up an office on his own, specializing in interior, exhibition, and furniture design. His work includes the Georg Jensen stores in New York and London, the Danish ambassador's residence in Washington, USA, and the SAS airline ticket offices around the globe. However, Juhl is best known today for his furniture designs.

He discovered his talent while designing furniture for his own apartment. His most famous pieces include the distinctive Chieftain Chai (or Høvdingestolen), 1949, the two-seater Poet sofa, 1941, and the softly rounded Pelican chair, 1940. What makes them so remarkable is their sculpted, flowing lines, inspired by modern and classical art and sculpture as well as traditional crafts. The Chieftain chair, for example, took direct inspiration from the sculpted shapes of African tribal shields. On Juhl's own notice-board, close to his desk at home, there still hangs some of his beautiful technical drawings alongside the sources of his inspiration, such as photographs of Greek temples and strips of cloth.

His organic, tactile, and sometimes voluptuous furniture was often made using exotic woods such as teak, maple, cherry, and

← This early fitted kitchen is in the Flerfamilijhus and was designed by architect Ralph Erskine. Its simple, practical style still looks good today.

↑ This elegant and delightful home was designed in 1942 by Danish furniture designer Finn Juhl. The light-filled living room features some of his furniture, including the classic Poet couch, which sits under a portrait of Juhl's partner Hanne Wilhelm Hansen, painted by Vilhelm Lundstrøm. Just visible in the foreground is Juhl's Cheftain chair of 1949.

← The exterior of Juhl's home, just outside Copenhagen, is a remarkably visionary piece of design from the 1940s, and one of just a handful of homes designed by him.

→ This double-cube storage cabinet, designed by Finn Juhl in 1974, has distinctive drawers finished in rainbow colours, and features scoop-shaped finger holes.

walnut. His pieces stand in stark contrast with those of many other designers of the time, who were working with rigid, straight, and geometric forms, and cheap, malleable beech wood. Juhl's work caused a considerable stir, cutting straight across the fashion for pared-down, basic, utility ware, but still remaining unmistakably modern. At a time when most other people were designing for factory production, Juhl concentrated on handcrafted items and for more than two decades worked alongside the cabinetmaker Niels Vodder. Despite this, many designs were also taken up for mass-production, and the American company Baker Furniture proved to be one enthusiastic manufacturer.

Painting and sculpture provided Juhl with such a constant source of inspiration that it is fitting that a painting provided the starting point for the 1942 design of his home. The painting from which he drew his inspiration was a late 1930s abstract still life by the Cubist Vilhelm Lundstrøm. It features a bowl on a stem, two oranges, and a sequence of abstract shapes in terra cotta, bright orange, yellow, blue, and cream – colours that eventually provided the decorating palette for the house.

An example of this use of colour is the built-in bench seat, upholstered in a terra cotta-coloured fabric, which is behind a table with a cream-coloured top, sitting on a cream rug on whitewashed floorboards. Displayed on the table are organic-shaped teak bowls, which themselves appear to be part of an abstract composition. Around the table are the elegant easy chairs, Model NV-45 from 1945. The tapered legs, shaped bracing bars, and neatly sculpted armrests invite you to touch, feel, and enjoy their smooth, rounded shapes. These chairs are typical of the many collaborations between Juhl and Niels Vodder, which also often featured experiments with new construction techniques. Not surprisingly these pieces have become highly collectable. In the 1960s and '70s, after the first early successes of his career, Juhl began to take life at a less frenetic pace, but he did continue to add to his personal furniture collection at home. One of his last pieces is a small storage cabinet with rainbow-coloured drawers, designed in 1974 as part of a modular storage system.

Juhl and his partner, Hanne Wilhelm Hansen, whom he met in 1960, were avid art collectors. It was a happy coincidence, therefore, that one of the paintings she brought with her when she moved in with him was a portrait of herself, completed when she was a teenager, by the artist Vilhelm Lundstrøm – the same painter of the Cubist still life that inspired the design of the entire house.

← This light-filled interior is given added interest by landscaping through changes of floor level. Built-in furniture includes display cases for favourite objects and comfortable window seats. Floors are left as plain scrubbed boards, finished with colourful, geometric-patterned rugs.

lighting with electricity

Winter days in Nordic countries can be incredibly short, sometimes stretching to just a few hours of meagre daylight. The Fins even have a word, "kaamos", to describe the deep winter days when there is hardly any daylight at all. As a result of this, there has been a prolific outpouring of ingenious Scandinavian lighting designs.

Among the first to demonstrate an understanding of electric light was the Danish designer Poul Henningsen, who produced his first works as early as the 1920s. He also had a social agenda, and believed in making functional objects beautiful and affordable. He thought that modern design should "promote architecture (and design) in accordance with the best of social, economic, and technological endeavours in modern culture". Henningsen's designs involve lightshades that are composed of a number of overlapping elements. By using calculations to work out how the light would interact with different shapes, he managed to reflect and diffuse the harsh light of a naked bulb. His career was based on a 40-year collaboration with the manufacturer Louis Poulsen. Among his most enduring designs are the 1957 PH Artichoke pendant lampshade and the 4-shade, designed in the late 1920s.

Louis Poulsen became established in the lighting business in 1892 by supplying fittings for Copenhagen's first power station. The company soon became established as one of Scandinavia's leading lamp producers when it employed the talents of designers such as Henningsen, followed by Arne Jacobsen, Verner Panton, and, more recently, contemporary designers such as Alfred Homann.

In Norway, the Luxo company became synonymous with lamp design. It was founded by lighting designer Jacob Jacobsen in the 1930s, when he acquired the Scandinavian production rights to the Anglepoise lamp by British designer George Carwadine. In 1937 Jacobsen designed his own, slightly softer, version of the lamp, the Luxo L-1, which became a huge bestseller and continues to be produced to this day – more than 25 million have been sold.

Scandinavian countries continue to produce intriguing new designs. Most recently these include the abstract and glowing "blocks" and "balls" of light by Finnish glass designer and artist Brita Flander, the highly memorable Block Lamp – simply a light-bulb set in a block of glass – by Finnish designer Harri Koskinen for the Swedish company Design House, and from Louis Poulsen the contemporary park lights and bollards by Alfred Homann.

← Natural light is reflected all around this white interior. It is enhanced by reflections in the glossy table top and the white ceramic tiling on the storage unit, which also contains the sink.

→ Alvar Aalto's studio, in the Helsinki suburb of Munkkiniemi, features a great double-height room. This was used as Aalto's office where he held meetings and tested his prototype light fittings, which still hang in situ today.

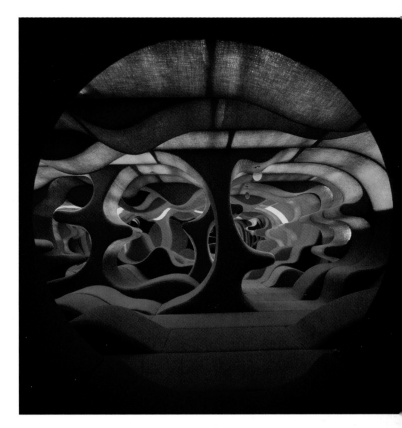

designs for the new world

Since the 1950s, when the Scandinavian Modern style received worldwide recognition, there has been an enduring fascination for its optimistic and elegant furniture, ceramics, lighting, glass, and silverware. Scandinavian style was quickly taken up in the USA. Visitors to the New York World Fair of 1939 were astonished by the radical design of the Finnish Pavilion, and well-known Scandinavian architects, Alvar Aalto included, had begun to lecture at universities all over the States. There were also touring exhibitions of Scandinavian products. The most famous was the Design in Scandinavia show, which, in January 1954, began its tour of almost two dozen museums throughout the USA and Canada. All this combined to whet the appetites of design and architecture aficionados, particularly the new generation of West Coast architects who shared the Scandinavian ideals.

The famous Californian Case Study houses of the 1940s and '50s were simple, modern homes for an informal lifestyle. Many used a rectangular box shape, incorporated exciting expanses of glass, and featured open-plan interiors. It is also possible to see a powerful Japanese influence. At the same time, the Scandinavian look had mass appeal – post-war America chose to furnish its new homes in Scandinavian style. Shops like Georg Jensen on Fifth Avenue were considered the height of chic, and, in 1960, when

Jackie Kennedy bought seven Marimekko outfits from a store in Cape Cod, Scandi-cool was established.

Along with the star architects, numerous great designer names have emerged – in Denmark, for example, Nanna Ditzel has long been a prolific furniture designer and is noted for her elegant designs. She has also produced stunning, organic-shaped silver jewellery for Georg Jensen, along with tableware and textiles. One of her most famous designs is the ceiling-suspended, egg-shaped, woven cane chair of 1957, but she is equally well-known for her expressive plywood furniture. Among the most startling and joyful of these designs is the Trinidad, 1993, made from two shaped discs of ply each featuring a cut-out sunburst design, and the famous Bench for Two, 1989, made of two linked armchairs with ply backrests finished with dazzling concentric circles. Her pioneering techniques in bending and moulding plywood have encouraged a new generation to experiment with the material.

Meanwhile, fellow Dane Verner Panton has enjoyed a huge renaissance of interest in his brightly coloured, moulded-plastic designs. Among his most iconic chairs is the 1959 Panton – a moulded swirl of plastic from its sculpted seat to the flared base. His trippy Phantasy Landscape is often used to sum up the essence of the 1960s; it is a part-furniture-part-architecture environment made of multicoloured, upholstered waves for lying or sitting on.

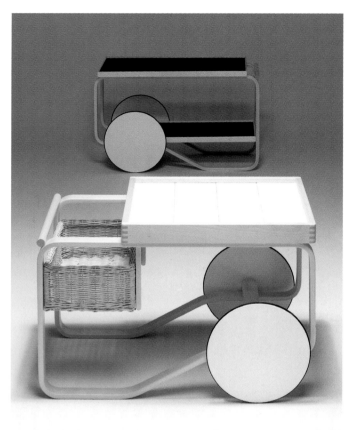

It is certainly a remarkable endorsement of the greatest Scandinavian designers that many of their products have not only succeeded in looking great decades after they were first produced, but that they are still in production and continue to appeal to new generations of home-makers all over the world.

Some of these design classics date way back to the 1930s, but look as good in the most minimal of loft apartments as they do in a comfortable family home. Finnish architect Alvar Aalto is, without doubt, one of those evergreen designers, and his chairs, tables, stools, lamps, and glassware form an amazing body of work. His wavy Savoy vase, designed in 1936 as part of a whole interior for Helsinki's Savoy restaurant, is perhaps the most instantly recognizable of all Scandinavian Modern objects. The Savoy interior is impressive too, and is still intact and in use to this day. Dozens of Aalto's designs, many made in collaboration with his first wife Aino Aalto, continue to be manufactured by Artek. This company was founded in 1935 to cope with growing numbers of export orders, which, at that time, came largely from Britain as the result of an Aalto exhibition at London's Fortnum and Mason store.

While Aalto was hard at work in Finland, the Danish designer and architect Arne Jacobsen produced his own series of startling designs, which are still in production today. Since it was first created, well over five million of the famous moulded and shaped plywood Ant chair have been sold, and the sexy, shapely Series 7 has become one of the most copied of all 20th-century chairs. Amazingly, both were designed more than half a century ago. Over his career Jacobsen's output has been quite staggering. Along with dozens of houses and numerous public buildings, banks, theatres, a hotel, and so on, he also has an astonishing track record in product design. He is responsible for many design classics, from beautiful chairs and lamps to tea and coffee sets, and the sleek stainless steel cutlery, Model No 600 AJ, which had a starring role in Stanley Kubrick's cult sci-fi film *2001: A Space Odyssey*.

In lighting there can be few greater names in 20th-century design than Poul Henningsen. This Danish designer started to design lamps in the 1920s, and was among the first to realise the potential of beautiful artificial lighting. He blended aesthetics with a scientific approach, his trademarks being the many layers of reflectors and diffusers that he used to soften and spread the fall of light. His collaboration with the manufacturer Louis Poulsen was an incredibly fruitful one, producing a clutch of design classics in the PH series of lamps and shades.

← (far left) The Tank armchair, with moulded, laminated birch sides, 1936, and the Tea Trolley, also of moulded, laminated birch, 1937, both designed by Alvar Aalto. It is likely that his wife Aino also helped in this work as creative director of the design office for Artek – the company founded to manufacture Aalto's designs.

← PH Artichoke lamp designed in 1957 by Poul Henningsen for lighting manufacturer Louis Poulsen. The cleverly layered "leaves" of this design demonstrate Henningsen's great understanding of how to soften and reflect the glare from an electric bulb.

↓ The sexy Series 7 chair by Arne Jacobsen, 1955. This design was remarkable for its day, using new moulding and shaping techniques to make a chairback and seat from a single piece of plywood.

← Arne Jacobsen's softly sculpted Swan chair, one of the many items, along with the Egg chair, that he designed for the SAS Royal Hotel in Copenhagen in the late 1950s. The extremely comfortable Swan chairs are still used in the hotel's lobby today.

row house – copenhagen, denmark

After decades of experiencing declining populations, as people left the hostile, crime-ridden, run-down city centres for a better quality of life in the suburbs, urban living has once again become desirable. Many Scandinavian cities have expended a huge effort into cleaning up the streets, investing in run-down areas, encouraging businesses back into the centres, and improving public transport systems. People have once again fallen in love with their towns and cities, and are happy to swap a life of commuting for the opportunity to walk or cycle to work. What is more, this style of living is not just finding favour with young professionals – it is also drawing in families and older people.

The area close to the centre of Copenhagen where Christian and Signe Cold, from the architecture practice Entasis, have their home was, for decades, completely out of fashion. It was run down and had few local amenities. "But it is only ten minutes from the centre of town," points out Signe Cold. It is also close to a lake, and the large park that contains the national gallery. However, since Copenhagen has smartened itself up, so their house and its surrounding area has become much sought-after.

Unusually for Copenhagen, the house is part of a terrace, having taken its inspiration from English terraced housing, and was built in 1875 for city workers. In those days it was on the edge of town, but it has long since been leap-frogged by subsequent expansion. The Danish describe this style of design as a row house, and this particular terrace is nicknamed "potato row". Although it has a floor area of only 135 square metres (1,450 square feet), it would originally have been occupied by three families, one on each floor – a total of perhaps 12 to 15 people. The fate of many of these houses has mirrored attitudes to city living and planning. "For example in the 1960s they were almost condemned and pulled down to

↓ (left) The simple living room is decorated in neutral colours and furnished with design classics – a chrome and leather sofa by Le Corbusier and side chairs by Poul Kjærholm.

↓ (right) The main bedroom on the top floor is fitted under the sloping eaves. The elegant bathing stand is clad in white ceramic mosaic tiles. This monumental element contains all the plumbing and runs through the centre of the house, concluding on the ground floor in the fireplace in the kitchen – also clad in the same mosaic tiles.

→ The ground floor kitchen, dining, and living area of this Danish terrace house opens onto a pretty courtyard. The impressive and monumental fireplace was designed by one of the owners, architect Christian Cold of Entasis. The inbuilt storage system contains a design classic, Royal Copenhagen china, and suspended from the ceiling is an Ikea chandelier.

↑ The children have their own entire floor in the middle of the house, which includes a play area, space for storing toys and books, and room for sleeping.

make way for radical new traffic systems," explains Christian Cold. "Then in the 1970s and '80s they became popular with academics. In the '90s they became hot property because they are so close to the centre; several politicians moved in and, of course, lots of architects."

When the Colds bought the building it was in a very run-down condition. The exterior is listed and could not be altered but, says Signe Cold, "we gutted everything, and kept the basic layout of rooms but opened up everywhere". Where the house had once been divided into 12 very small rooms, it has now become one flowing space.

The family's living area is situated on the ground floor; a new kitchen was installed and a handsome black metal fireplace was designed by Christian. The kitchen area is clad entirely in white porcelain mosaic from Portugal, and opens onto a much-loved sunny courtyard; to help the inside and outside spaces flow together, the level of the yard was lowered to meet the level of the kitchen floor, both of which are finished in concrete.

The floor directly above the living area has been set aside for the children and consists of a playroom and bedroom. The top floor is a peaceful retreat for the grown-ups. Their bedroom sits under the sloping roof, but is well-lit by generous dormer windows. It also features an unusual washstand in the form of a simple, monumental block clad in the same white porcelain mosaic tiles that feature in the kitchen. The use of the mosaic tiles runs from top to bottom through a central core – below the washstand in the parents' bedroom is located the children's bathroom and storage unit, and then below that again is the kitchen area with its wall-mounted, custom-made fire.

In keeping with the idea of flowing and overlapping space, furniture and clutter throughout the house is kept to a minimum wherever possible. The furniture includes classic pieces by famous designers such as Charles and Ray Eames, Le Corbusier, Harry Bertoia, and Poul Kjærholm.

↓ The children's zone includes inbuilt storage. This is clad in the same white ceramic mosaic tiles as those found in the parents' bedroom above, and the living area below.

→ There is a mix of old and new in this city-centre apartment. The original decorative plasterwork on the ceiling has been retained, while the room below is furnished with a contemporary L-shaped sofa and a classic, black leather Swan chair designed in the late 1950s by Danish master Arne Jacobsen.

↑ A black, white, and grey decorative theme has been used in this large Danish apartment. Steel stairs rise to the mezzanine level above, while below, the built-in storage, with its clever lighting, has a strong sculptural quality. The wood-burning stove brings a glow of warmth, light, and colour to the room.

historical spaces

Because Scandinavian cities were not damaged by bombing during World War II, much of the fabric of the older buildings remains very well preserved. There is also little empty building space left in city centres and, consequently, it is rare to see entirely new structures rising in the hearts of the cities. This means that for many people who want to live close to the centre of the cities, the homes and apartments that are available to them are likely to be at least a century old. As a result, the inhabitants of these old houses must fit their contemporary living styles into homes that were designed for an entirely different age and way of living. On the positive side, many of the great mansion blocks of the late 19th and early 20th centuries contain generous apartments, with tall rooms that provide large and fairly flexible living spaces. Unfortunately there are still plenty of dark apartments with small windows, and the heavy style of decoration that was popular in the past. The response of many has been to entirely gut these spaces and reduce them to a desirable white box; against this neutralized backdrop it is then possible to import modern furniture and to impose a contemporary way of life.

The grandest Scandinavian apartments are just about as close as it gets to the style of loft living that was first made so popular in the USA. It is still rare in Scandinavian cities to see residential development taking place in former industrial areas, with warehouses and factories being converted into houses and apartments. These cities have yet to feel the pressure to provide homes for people wanting to move in, and the supply of existing housing is still able to meet demand. However, there are small schemes underway in pockets of Copenhagen and Stockholm, where former industrial buildings are being transformed into offices, clubs, restaurants, and new homes. The Holmen area, a former military base in Copenhagen's harbour, is one such example of this type of urban redevelopment.

← Every scrap of space has been used in this Danish town house. The attic space has been opened up by the use of windows and doors in the gable-end wall, and with a roof light. The sculptural chair and stool are by the British designer Matthew Hilton.

↑ The neutral colour scheme is enlivened with bold splashes of colour provided by an abstract painting and a glowing red door with its over-sized steel handle.

← There is no better way of getting round Danish towns and cities than by bicycle. In this hallway the bicycle sits alongside a pair of classic moulded plastic chairs. Called the Panton, the chairs were designed by Danish designer Verner Panton and date from the early 1960s.

↑ The calmness of the space here is emphasized by the low-level furniture and shelving. The elegant chair and table are by the Danish furniture designer Poul Kjærholm. The chair is the Model no. PK22 from 1955; unlike many of his Danish contemporaries Kjærholm adopted steel, rather than wood, as his material of choice.

scandinavian love of wood

Even in the city Scandinavians love to feel that nature is never far away. Big urban areas generally feature a liberal sprinkling of parks and open spaces, and in smaller towns and cities it can take just minutes to escape into the countryside. This affinity with nature and natural things has always found a place in modern Scandinavian interiors – the pioneering Finnish architect Alvar Aalto regularly took inspiration from the natural world for the design of his products and buildings.

In this continuing urge to keep in touch with nature, timber has always been a major feature of Scandinavian interiors. All the pioneering modern architects – Alvar Aalto, Arne Jacobsen, Jørn Utzon – and the great furniture designers – Finn Juhl, Hans Wegner, and Nanna Ditzel – have been fascinated by the potential of wood, and have experimented continually with new forms of construction and manufacturing techniques. Aalto is

renowned for his laminated, curved chair frames, while Jacobsen and Ditzel have pushed the shaping and moulding of plywood to new heights and extremes.

One Scandinavian trademark is the use of timber in an untreated or unpainted state, so that it is possible to appreciate the natural colours and patterns. Sometimes it is left entirely untreated to age naturally and gracefully, in other cases it is finished with a coloured stain or an oil, both of which expose the grain and texture. Timber has always been one of Scandinavia's most plentiful raw materials, and forestry, in all but Denmark, continues to be a major industry. As a raw material, wood finds countless applications, from building timber-framed homes to paper production, furniture, and even the more unlikely uses, such as when wood is pulped and the strong fibre woven into rugs.

Over the years, careful management of the forests has ensured that there is a sustainable production of wood. Compared with a century ago there is around double the amount of timber growing in Scandinavia today. Two principal species are grown, the redwood or pine, and whitewood or spruce. Birch, which provides the supple, pale blonde wood that is used in the manufacture of so much furniture and plywood, as well as the making of musical instruments, is the next most popular. Throughout most of the world, Nordic timber is highly prized because its slow growth rate results in a dense, strong timber with small branches, which means that it has smaller knots. The better-quality Scandinavian woods come from the more northerly regions.

Both redwood and whitewood are used in construction, with the highest grades used for interior panels, windows, architraving, and finishes, such as flooring. More exotic timbers are also imported, but there remains a loyal following for locally grown materials.

scandinavian minimalism

For many people who choose to live in the heart of the city, there must be a compromise between quality of location and quantity of space. The general rule, unless you are incredibly wealthy, is that one is most often bought at the expense of the other. Quantity of space becomes even more of an issue for those who choose to live in central urban locations with their children, as it requires a certain skill and discipline to manage grown-ups and children, with all their possessions, in a limited space.

For Scandinavians this lack of urban space is nothing new. During the late 19th century, when the agricultural way of life was on the wane and people started streaming into the cities in search of employment, it was quite normal to be squeezed into incredibly cramped quarters. Whole families were jammed into a single room, and had to share facilities such as lavatories with numerous other families. They were grim years, made even tougher by sporadic outbreaks of disease, but stemming from that incredible hardship came the pledge that the people deserved better. Politicians and social reformers recoiled from the nightmare lives inflicted on poor people. Designers and architects started to devise ways of improving lives through better-quality designs, which encompassed bigger, lighter better-planned homes, as well as practical, versatile furniture, and good-quality lighting – all the elements that we recognize today as being typical to Scandinavian homes. Scandinavian designers, for example, were among the first to devise ingenious multipurpose and space-saving furniture – tables that transformed into sofas, sofas that became beds, chairs that could stack one on top of the other. The flat-pack furniture idea emerged here as early as the 1940s, so it is of little surprise that today's Scandinavian urban dwellers have plenty of skill in making the most of smaller spaces.

The Danish home featured on these pages is situated in an apartment block that was built in 1905, and is lived in by a couple and their one young child. When they took over the apartment it was dark and gloomy, the floors were carpeted, and the walls were painted in dark and dingy colours. However, the couple could see the potential, and decided to throw themselves into the project by entirely gutting and stripping the interior back to bare floors and walls. The original pine floorboards were then sanded and restored, and the walls were painted white in order to reflect the available light around the rooms.

Their ingenious and space-saving ideas start right at the front door with the two, tall, wall-fixed shoe storage boxes in the small entrance lobby. Bought from Ikea, the units have trays that flip down to open and flip up to make a closed box. It is a neat and simple idea that prevents the usual chaos of shoes around the door. The boxes also add a welcome blast of warm colour as you enter the apartment. Progressing further into the apartment, the furniture has been carefully chosen to be comfortable and yet not to fill the place. One of the owners, a designer, has created the solid, timber-built work table, and a matching pair of benches, to sit in one corner of the living area. The long lamp suspended over the table can be easily raised or lowered as required.

The main living and dining room is a serene space, which is again decorated in white. The sound system is particularly important here, since the other owner works in the music industry and enjoys listening to music on high-quality equipment. However, the couple was well aware of one of the universal problems of inner-city living, that of

← The small hallway at the entrance of this apartment is painted white to reflect light around the enclosed space. A dash of colour is added in the form of a pair of neat, space-efficient, Ikea shoe cupboards.

↓ The table and bench arrangement in this apartment was designed by one of the owners. The long pendant table lamp can be raised or lowered when necessary.

↑ The dining area has a distinctive space-age feel. The unusual moulded glass fibre chairs and table are by Eero Saarinen and sit under a "futuristic" pendant lamp. The collection of CDs is given a highly decorative treatment, stowed in nine boxes that appear to be suspended in space.

hearing other people's music. As there were so many large expanses of hard, sound-reflecting areas – walls, floors, and large windows – and no carpet, little padded furniture, and no heavy drapes to absorb the sound, they were concerned that the noise pollution problem was likely to have been exacerbated by their decision to decorate and furnish the flat in a minimalist style. The owners were reluctant to compromise their specific style of living, but at the same time they did want to be considerate to their neighbours. Their solution to the problem was a brilliant one.

Having done some research into how noisy places, such as recording studios and offices, cope with absorbing ambient sound, the couple discovered an insulating material called Rockfon Koral, which is usually used in suspended ceilings to deaden harsh sounds. By taking a single large panel of the material, and cleverly disguising it as the painting that hangs over the sofa, they created a sound barrier. Although it is just a single panel, it has proved to be incredibly effective at soaking up noise and it enables the couple to enjoy their music without disturbing their neighbours. The rug in front of the sofa also helps a little in absorbing some of the sound. By coming up with this ingenious idea the couple have managed to ensure that their interior design remains uncompromised, and the simplicity of space, even down to the light cotton drapes at the French windows, is just as they wanted it.

Music is clearly celebrated in this apartment in other ways – close to the 1950s dining table and moulded, glass-fibre dining chairs by Finnish architect Eero Saarinen, there is an unusually decorative collection of CD shelving units. Almost like an art installation, nine boxes are fixed to the wall in a square pattern. The idea is picked up on another wall where more units contain books. The 1950s theme of this area is completed with a swirling, white, Le Klint pendant lamp shade, which hovers over the table.

↓ The living area is calm and restrained, and sunlight is filtered through light, muslin drapes at the large French windows. The painting above the sofa is in fact a panel of super-sound-absorbent material, which helps to soak up noise from the owners' sophisticated music system.

pattern and texture

In decorating schemes where simplicity and elegance rule, and the palette of colours and materials is highly restrained, the introduction of pattern and texture must be judged with great care. Like loud sounds in a quiet place, every new addition can draw attention to itself, so extreme care must be taken when introducing something different.

The contemporary Scandinavian style, in tune with international tastes, is based on a minimalist approach. Its focus is on reducing rooms to their simplest form, making the most of space and light, and providing an uncluttered and calm backdrop for busy lives. This inevitably leads to rooms that are finished with large expanses of plain, sheer materials, so the quality of the materials and the skill with which they are installed is incredibly important. A small area of damage or a smudge of dirt on a sheer white wall immediately attracts the eye; we become hypersensitive to blemishes because expectations are raised to see a perfect sheer white wall. It can be an unforgiving environment, as simplicity can be extremely hard to achieve and equally hard to maintain.

Inside such a highly finished white box, the choice of materials will set the tone of the place – for example, in the same room, a floor with a plain vinyl or carpet covering will have quite a different feel from a floor with highly polished or oiled oak boards. In many ways the Scandinavian handling of materials can be compared with the Japanese. There is an incredible sensitivity, especially when using natural materials like wood and stone; they are treated as if they are precious, used in sparing amounts, and always to emphasize their natural beauty, whether it is the grain in wood or the weave of linen. These pleasures and subtleties are lost in interiors that are crowded with pattern and texture.

This approach to design also makes it possible to find beauty in the most unexpected places. In the Copenhagen apartment, shown opposite, the owners, architect Rikke Haugaard and photographer Casper Sejersen, stripped away all the old decorative finishes when they were refurbishing the interior. Working with high-ceilinged, spacious rooms, they wanted to create the feeling of a loft-style apartment. As the layers of wallpaper and coats of paint were removed, they revealed an intriguing patchwork of raw plaster and filler on the wall beneath. Its abstract quality appealed to the owners, who decided to make a virtue of their discovery. They decorated the rest of the flat white but left one large panel of wall untouched. The unconscious, free-form patinated effect is celebrated by being framed by a white-painted wall. The raw pattern and texture is set alongside the luxury and richness of a dark leather armchair, which has been draped with a soft blanket. In the centre of the room sits the plain wood refectory-style dining table, by Blå Station, with its retro basket-weave chairs. A delicate touch has been added with the paper pendant lampshades and the almost transparent, long, muslin curtains. Like the very best recipes, every texture can be appreciated in its own right. Elsewhere in the apartment the white theme continues, with colour being added in small splashes – in paintings, plants, and in small items of furniture.

While the coolest Scandinavian minimalism incorporates the use of natural materials and textures, man-made pattern is often left out of the equation. However, numerous Scandinavian designers have produced patterns of unusual and extraordinary beauty, and many of the Modernist architectural pioneers turned their hand to designing fabrics. Danish

← This intriguing wall panel is actually a section of the wall as it was discovered when the owners Rikke Haugaard, architect, and Casper Sejersen, photographer, stripped off the layers of old paint and wallpaper. They liked the effect so much they decided to leave it, and painted around it. The table is by Blå Station.

↓ The high-ceilinged apartment is painted entirely white, including fixed objects such as the wall-hung, open storage system. Accent colour is introduced using small pieces of furniture and paintings.

master Arne Jacobsen, for example, designed several, surprisingly floral, textile and wallpaper patterns. One of the most architectural in style is a stylish fabric print called Rushes; made in Sweden, it shows tall stylized rush grasses against a plain background and it dates from the early 1940s. The Finn Alvar Aalto worked on more abstract and geometric patterns, and some of his fabrics are still in production to this day.

One of the most prolific of the early pattern designers was Josef Frank, who worked for Swedish interiors company Svenskt Tenn. Frank was Austrian, but he went to work in Sweden in the 1930s, and soon after adopted Swedish nationality. As chief designer of Svenskt Tenn he produced designs for a huge range of interior wares, from furniture to fabrics. However, it was for his fabrics that he was rediscovered at the start of the 21st century. Being a keen amateur botanist and fascinated by plants, almost all of his designs are based on patterns from nature. Sometimes, as in the upholstered bench shown in the photograph opposite, they are abstract, flowing organic designs, while in other instances they are highly detailed, figurative depictions. Large numbers of these designs, although originally created in the 1930s and '40s, continue to be produced by Svenskt Tenn today.

In the post-war years, Scandinavian fabric designs and the craft weavers have drawn appreciative audiences worldwide. Great names include the Danes Lis Ahlmann and Vibeke Klint, who produced exquisite geometric-patterned textiles and rugs; Swedish designers Stig Lindberg and Sven Markelius, who were among those producing wonderful abstract Modernist fabric designs for the famous Nordiska Kompaniet department store; and the Finn Vuokko Nurmesniemi, hailed as "Finland's first fashion designer". Although Vuokko

↓ The owner of this apartment is a clothes designer who enjoys experimenting with textures. Here, the sleek curved plywood of the modern chair by Charles and Ray Eames is joined by the natural wood table and richly coloured cushions in silk and cotton.

→ The fabric on this upholstered bench is by the Austrian designer Josef Frank, who joined the famous Swedish interior design company Svenskt Tenn in the mid-1930s. He was prolific, producing furniture as well as textiles – many of which are still made. Frank was a keen botanist, and this fabric is typical of his textile designs, which take their inspiration from organic forms and colours in nature.

first worked as a ceramic designer for the well-known Finnish company Arabia, she changed direction in her early twenties when she became artistic director at Marimekko, Scandinavia's best-known textile design and fashion house. Married to the product designer and architect Antti Nurmesniemi, she saw it as her mission to drive out the dreary black and brown clothes of post-war Finland, and set out to make Marimekko a home of vibrant and easy-to-wear clothing. After Marimekko's first fashion show in the USA, one newspaper journalist was so struck by the bright colours and bold patterns they described Nurmesniemi as "Finland's Matisse". Among her most famous fabric designs are the stripy Piccolo textiles of the 1950s. Today, Nurmesniemi runs her own fashion house Vuokko, selling modern classic clothing.

As a refreshing diversion from the restrained and quiet good taste of textiles in geometric patterns and neutral colours, the Finn Maija Isola set out to dazzle and shock her

↓ This room demonstrates a clever fusion of contemporary design with crafts. The masks were brought home from Tanzania and Kenya, and their dark colour is picked up in the dark-stained oak sideboard. Meanwhile, the easy chair, with its woven back and seat, is a 1949 design by the Dane Hans Wegner.

audience. Her most famous design is Unikko, or Poppy, which she created in 1960 for Marimekko. This bold, abstract, and brightly coloured design is hard to beat for sheer exuberance and fun, and continues to appeal to new generations of home-makers all over the world. Her other famous designs include the parallel squiggles of Lokki, or Seagull, and the rounded forms of Melooni, or Melon.

The Scandinavian textile tradition continues in the early 21st century with fabrics that are richly textured, and produced either in natural colours or vivid primaries. Currently, one of the most sought-after designers is the Swede Pia Wallén. She has explored the textural and sculptural qualities of various materials, but one of her fascinations has been for felt and her simple felt slippers, with distinctive contrasting stitching, have become classics. She is also renowned for her Dot carpets and the bold, primary-coloured Krux, or Cross, blankets and rugs.

↑ The stained oak chosen for the built-in cupboards throughout this apartment was also used to make this bed. The wonderfully uplifting and colourful duvet cover is the Unikko, or Poppy, design, made by Maija Isola in 1960 for the Finnish company Marimekko.

↓ (Overleaf) This large, open-plan apartment, by architects Kjellander and Sjoberg, has been created from a converted 1938 orphanage at Södermalm, just south of Stockholm. Much of the structure has survived intact, including the original wood windows with their granite window ledges. The lighting is by the manufacturer Flos, with a sofa by Swedish designer Eero Koivisto.

↑ This elegant family town house is furnished with simple, contemporary pieces, including a pair of easy chairs, Model no. PK22 from 1955, by Danish furniture designer Poul Kjærholm. The height of the space is given emphasis by keeping all furnishings at low level, so everything fits below the line of the window ledge.

open-plan living

It would be reasonable to expect homes in a cold climate to be divided into a series of small, cosy, easy-to-heat rooms. However, the contemporary Scandinavian interior is anything but closed. The open-plan concept has been a constant theme in interiors throughout the 20th century, and it continues to be one today. The appeal of the open-plan space is not only that it provides greater flexibility in terms of layout, and it makes much better use of floor space than a home divided into rooms, but that it also provides the opportunity for precious natural light to be drawn into the heart of buildings.

Many designs, including those from early on in the 20th century, have evolved subtle ways of marking spaces within an open-plan layout, while maintaining the unhindered flow of light. This can be achieved in numerous ways: with changes of floor level to make a sunken seating area or raised dining podium, or with the use of freestanding screens, or small areas of wall. Less permanent features, such as rugs, can also be used to define an area. In a large space, for example, a rug underneath the seating or dining area will make it obvious that the areas to the side of the rug are meant for circulation. To ensure that these open interiors are comfortable and warm, Scandinavian design has for decades led the world in their high levels and methods of insulating against the cold, which include double- and triple-glazed windows, and wall and roof insulation.

Another feature of open-plan, contemporary interior design is the use of streamlined, low-level furniture and fittings. When this sort of furniture is used, the long, horizontal lines achieve a calming effect on the feel of the space. Low-level furniture also has the illusion of making rooms appear taller and airier than they often are, as it does not act as a block to any of the precious light coming into the room.

↓ Spaces flow together seamlessly, but also succeed in having a degree of separation provided by slices of wall. Here the wall provides a screen between the hall and living room.

socializing spaces

Scandinavians are generally noted for their hospitality, so they see their homes as social places where friends and family regularly get together to socialize and exchange news and gossip. As with so many aspects of Scandinavian life, the climate also plays a role here. Whereas life in a warm climate, such as the Mediterranean, is often lived out on the street and in cafés, in the cooler north people choose to entertain their friends and family at home. There can be no doubt that this has had an large impact on contemporary interior planning in Nordic countries. "The move in recent years has definitely been towards larger and more open living spaces, which has meant sleeping areas have tended to become smaller," says Per Axelsson of Stockholm-based Nyréns Arkitektkontor. "But always the kitchen is a generous size – this is where everyone meets and talks. Storage space is also an essential component in any interior plan – there has to be cupboard-room for large items such as skis, winter clothing, and any other bulky items that might fill up the home. Keeping living areas clutter free is a high priority. Because winters are so long and we spend a lot of time inside, we don't want to choke the spaces with possessions, the minimalist approach is in our culture," says Axelsson.

The home featured on these pages is in a newly built, low-rise apartment block on the Stockholm waterside in Sweden. The building is contemporary in style, and, true to the environmentally sound Scandinavian ethos, features solar cells on the roof that produce as much as 15 per cent of the building's electricity needs. The interior was specifically designed for a young professional couple, who like to invite friends for supper and parties. The simple layout includes a large living space, which opens to one side into the large kitchen, and opposite into a bedroom. The furnishing has been kept simple, clean, and contemporary, being finished in white accented with zesty orange details.

↓ This open-plan living space is designed for sociable urban dwellers who like entertaining friends. Space engineering in contemporary apartments has now moved towards larger living areas and smaller sleeping spaces.

minimalist apartment – stockholm, sweden

"Building for oneself is interesting," contemplates Swedish architect Mårten Claesson. "On the one hand you don't have to go through the whole persuasion/compromise process. On the other hand you tend never to be satisfied. You have to consider it more an ongoing experiment than an actual project in order to be able to go ahead." Claesson is part of the Claesson Koivisto Rune partnership, which is renowned for its work in extending and exploring the ideas of Minimalism, and producing refined and sleek interiors and furniture.

Claesson's small apartment had been a single floor at the top level of an apartment block. In remodelling the space, he incorporated the previously unused attic space and stripped the entire apartment. "Even though it is on two floors, the idea was to make a single, flowing space," explains Claesson, adding that there is now just one door in the whole apartment – for the bathroom. "The different areas for cooking, eating, and sleeping are defined, but they interlock and flow together". The lower level now contains the public spaces of kitchen, dining, and living, with the private spaces for sleeping and working located upstairs. Connecting the two levels is a minimal white stairway, fitted into the wall that divides the dining and living areas. The slender, white-painted metal treads are cantilevered from the wall – the supporting structure is embedded behind the plaster.

The apartment is painted white throughout, with white-stained oak flooring downstairs and wool carpet upstairs. It is lightly furnished. "The space is small, so I have only what I need," says Claesson. Furniture includes a number of prototypes designed by the architect, including a cedar-wood bathtub, an easy chair, a telephone table, and dining table in oiled elm, together with the elegant beech work table and chair from the Lite series, and a walnut chair and futon bed in the bedroom.

↓ (left) This flight of white stairs appears to defy gravity to simply hang in space. In order to achieve this look, each step is cantilevered from the wall.

↓ (right) The sleeping area is simply furnished with a futon bed, which has been custom designed by Claesson, and his Bend chair, made in walnut. The white painting is by Brian Wendleman, and the white, plastic wall clock is called Camp and is by David Design.

→ This is the roof-space work area in the apartment of Swedish architect Mårten Claesson of Claesson Koivisto Rune. Sitting under the window is the pale beech wood work table and chair from the Lite series by Claesson. Standing on the floor is the AJ lamp from Louis Poulsen, designed in 1957 by Arne Jacobsen.

converted school house – southern sweden

Although the spare and sparsely furnished rooms of this Swedish home have the feeling of a contemporary city apartment, they have in fact been created in a converted school in the countryside of southern Sweden. The interior was designed by leading architecture practice Claesson Koivisto Rune for the highly respected glass and ceramics designer Ingegerd Råman and her artist husband Claes Söderquist.

Originally, the school was divided into two classrooms and a gymnasium. The refurbishment plan was to clear the space entirely in order to make a large, ground-floor kitchen, with separate dining and living area, plus a studio space where Råmen could continue with her work from home. Upstairs there would be a main bedroom suite and guest bedroom. In converting an old rural building like this, it might have been expected to take an approach that would have produced a soft, traditionally styled interior, "But the client was not looking for a traditional feel to the place," explains Mårten Claesson. "She is very well known for her extremely precise and restrained glassware designs, and that was the approach we took to this space."

Råman is one of Sweden's best-known glass designers and is noted for her work with Swedish glass manufacturers Skruf and Orrefors. Her designs for items such as bowls, vases, and water flasks are elemental, almost disarmingly simple, but always the product of a rigorous approach to high-quality and extremely fine detailing. One of her most noted trademarks is the dual functionality of her designs, for example her series called Jar is a range of containers that can be used as fruit bowls, vases, or water jugs. She is also known for incorporating exciting, thoughtful details – her water flask called Chambermaid has, as its top, an upturned drinking glass that continues the flowing line of the side of the flask. In another practical design, this time for an olive oil carafe, the round glass stopper has one flat side to prevent it from rolling away.

The school, built in brick and given a white stucco finish, had been disused for more than four decades, so the first step was to clear the space. Ten huge containers of old panelling, doors, wiring, and rubbish were filled. "We wanted to uncover and keep the old fabric of the building just as it was, virtually untouched, so that it provided a strong contrast with the new elements," explains Claesson.

The first visual clue to the school's stunning transformation is to be found at the front door – leading up to it is a flight of elegantly modern concrete steps. "They are no more than a couple of inches thick and appear to be folded into shape, like cardboard," says Claesson. Inside, the stripped space is finished with smooth plastering, and the flooring has been replaced with bleached and white-oiled pine. To maintain the clean, airy flow of the rooms, they are minimally furnished; the sleek, white kitchen is also in keeping with this look and is constructed from a Finnish system by the manufacturer Saari. In order to achieve the stripped, bare interior, a major clear out of all extraneous materials, including panelling, skirting, and doors, was involved.

Despite their early plans to incorporate a studio within the space, the clients decided that they loved the minimal interior so much they wanted to keep it free from the mess of work. They therefore decided to commission the architects to design and build a separate studio in the grounds of the school.

↓ The gutted interior of this former country school now provides a sequence of intriguing abstract views through the spaces. Here, looking up the dark flight of stairs, the upper floors open into light and airy rooms. The architect for this project was Claesson Koivisto Rune.

↑ This contemporary kitchen has been carved from classrooms in this converted school house in the south of Sweden. The white kitchen system is by the Finnish manufacturer Saari. The flooring is bleached and white-oiled pine.

contemporary office – stockholm, sweden

The light and airy spaces, large windows, sleek minimal kitchen, white furniture, and oak wood flooring make this the kind of city apartment that most urban dwellers dream about. It is in fact home to the small but well-known media agency Audumbla, and stands as an example of how the design of home and work environments have merged in recent years – while people at work want the comforts of home, people at home want the contemporary designs of the office. "The design idea was to create an environment that felt welcoming, relaxed, and very much like a home; like coming to a friend's modern private apartment," explains Mårten Claesson of architecture practice Claesson Koivisto Rune.

The interior incorporates many of the elements for which the practice has become well known, including the stripped bare walls, usually painted white but in this case given a grey, ceramic, mosaic finish in the kitchen area. The kitchen is in a simple, monumental style system by Saari of Finland, with flat-fronted doors and no handles to distract the eye; while it is used for making drinks and snacks, most of the cupboards are used as office storage space. Visitors to the office are greeted in the main living space, but beyond there are frosted-glass partitions that mark out three small offices. These semi-private areas stand in place of what might have been bedrooms in a private apartment.

Much of the furniture and fittings was designed by the architects, but there are also chairs by Arne Jacobsen, a sofa by Piero Lissoni, a coffee table and meeting table by Monica Armani, and an orange rug by Pia Wallén. An interesting extra detail is the night-time lighting. "The company is based in a 1930s Modernist office building, which stands on a hill slightly above Stockholm city centre and can be seen from a long way," describes Claesson. "And while Audumbla didn't want to have its name up in lights we have made the place a landmark by adding red lighting in a trough at the top of the windows – at night the place is flooded with red light, which can clearly be seen from the street."

↑ The home-from-home feeling of this workplace is continued in the meeting area, where the soft white line sofa sits behind the white meeting table, with Myran, or Ant, chairs by Arne Jacobsen.

first worked as a ceramic designer for the well-known Finnish company Arabia, she changed direction in her early twenties when she became artistic director at Marimekko, Scandinavia's best-known textile design and fashion house. Married to the product designer and architect Antti Nurmesniemi, she saw it as her mission to drive out the dreary black and brown clothes of post-war Finland, and set out to make Marimekko a home of vibrant and easy-to-wear clothing. After Marimekko's first fashion show in the USA, one newspaper journalist was so struck by the bright colours and bold patterns they described Nurmesniemi as "Finland's Matisse". Among her most famous fabric designs are the stripy Piccolo textiles of the 1950s. Today, Nurmesniemi runs her own fashion house Vuokko, selling modern classic clothing.

As a refreshing diversion from the restrained and quiet good taste of textiles in geometric patterns and neutral colours, the Finn Maija Isola set out to dazzle and shock her audience. Her most famous design is Unikko, or Poppy, which she created in 1960 for Marimekko. This bold, abstract, and brightly coloured design is hard to beat for sheer exuberance and fun, and continues to appeal to new generations of home-makers all over the world. Her other famous designs include the parallel squiggles of Lokki, or Seagull, and the rounded forms of Melooni, or Melon.

The Scandinavian textile tradition continues in the early 21st century with fabrics that are richly textured, and produced either in natural colours or vivid primaries. Currently, one of the most sought-after designers is the Swede Pia Wallén. She has explored the textural and sculptural qualities of various materials, but one of her fascinations has been for felt and her simple felt slippers, with distinctive contrasting stitching, have become classics. She is also renowned for her Dot carpets and the bold, primary-coloured Krux, or Cross, blankets and rugs.

open-plan living

It would be reasonable to expect homes in a cold climate to be divided into a series of small, cosy, easy-to-heat rooms. However, the contemporary Scandinavian interior is anything but closed. The open-plan concept has been a constant theme in interiors throughout the 20th century, and it continues to be one today. The appeal of the open-plan space is not only that it provides greater flexibility in terms of layout, and it makes much better use of floor space than a home divided into rooms, but that it also provides the opportunity for precious natural light to be drawn into the heart of buildings.

Many designs, including those from early on in the 20th century, have evolved subtle ways of marking spaces within an open-plan layout, while maintaining the unhindered flow of light. This can be achieved in numerous ways: with changes of floor level to make a sunken seating area or raised dining podium, or with the use of freestanding screens, or small areas of wall. Less permanent features, such as rugs, can also be used to define an area. In a large space, for example, a rug underneath the seating or dining area will make it obvious that the areas to the side of the rug are meant for circulation. To ensure that these open interiors are comfortable and warm, Scandinavian design has for decades led the world in their high levels and methods of insulating against the cold, which include double- and triple-glazed windows, and wall and roof insulation.

→ The new living room occupies the attic space in this 1930s apartment block. Huge roof lights have been fitted to flood the space with sunlight. Furniture includes the distinctive steel-and-leather armchairs called Rex, which are by the designer Mats Theselius.

↓ The sculptural concrete fireplace was cast on site. It sits in the corner of the chimney breast and the shelf extends beyond the wall and into the room.

and heavy bath that the owner had chosen. Instead of using predictable ceramic tiling on the walls of this bathroom, the architect finished them in sheets of Swedish glass, back-lit by a phased lighting system that glows through the entire spectrum of colours. Other Swedish materials include black granite, which was used for the floors in the kitchen and bathroom, and a countertop in the kitchen that was constructed from Scandinavian, slow-grown birch, which has a particularly fine grained pattern.

Furnishing throughout the apartment is an eclectic mixture of modern classics and contemporary design. On the lower level, for example, the dining area has a large oval table with Arne Jacobsen dining chairs; the impressive pendant lamp suspended over the table came from the hallway of an old school. Moving up to the upper level, the theme becomes more loft-like and industrial, to match the style of the space and the details such as the concrete fireplace. The living room furniture includes a

↓ The dining area sits at the bottom of the cantilvered stairs. Around the oval table are Arne Jacobsen chairs, and suspended above is an unusual pendant lamp that once hung in the hall of an old school.

contemporary-style sofa and a pair of unusual steel and leather armchairs, called Rex, by Swedish designer/artist Mats Theselius. The steel sheeting on the armchairs was first given a nickel plating and then a matt chrome finish, while the interior leather was made in a single piece using shoemaking techniques on a last. Theselius is one of Sweden's best-known young designers, and has established a reputation for his provocative approach to design. In one exhibition, for example, he chose to focus on the country's dismal and ugly satellite towns – not something to be celebrated by a nation with a worldwide reputation for good design. He also bucks the trend of beautifully finished and crafted products by making furniture, like the Rex chairs, that has an edgy, almost rough finish. Designed in 1994, the full name of the chair is Theselius REX – "but nobody seems to understand the joke" he says. Just 200 of these chairs were made and all sold immediately – they are now highly collectable items.

← The spacious living room features a large, comfortable seating area that is marked out by the cream-coloured rug. The position of the rug leaves a clear floor space round the edge of the room for circulation.

↑ The library area is calm and contemplative, with its matching ochre-coloured armchairs by Claesson Koivisto Rune, and intriguing paper lampshade by the American sculptor and designer Isamu Noguchi.

← The huge dining table (4.5m/15ft long) was fashioned from a single African walnut tree-trunk. At the end of the dining room sits the altar-like kitchen. The room has a monochrome colour scheme, where the white is broken with the dramatic black of the dining chairs, dark-stained wood of the table, and the solid black granite worktops and black glass splash-back in the kitchen.

grand apartment – stockholm, sweden

In a dramatic bid to open up the spaces in this large apartment, the walls were taken down to transform the place from seven rooms into just three main, free-flowing spaces for sitting, cooking and eating, and sleeping. The handsome home, once the Soviet ambassador's residence in Stockholm, is on the third floor of a 1920s city-centre block and has windows on three sides, which provide plenty of sunlight. Once the owners had decided that they wanted to increase the airy and spacious feeling of the apartment, they asked leading architecture practice Claesson Koivisto Rune to work its magic.

The preparatory work entailed removing walls and stripping out some of the old interior – they left in place a great deal of the original plaster mouldings and decorative architraving "so that the new additions could be seen in clear contrast with the backdrop of the old" explains architect Mårten Claesson. The walls were painted white and the oak flooring was restored where it was damaged, and given a white-limed finish. The main in-built features include the library wall, complete with fireplace, the walnut bed, and the walnut-and-glass cased sauna in the bathroom. The bathroom floor had to be strengthened to take the weight of the beautiful bowl-shaped limestone bath, designed by Claudio Silvestrin for the manufacturer Boffi. Large items, including the bath and a 4.5 metre (15ft) walnut dining table, had to be craned into the flat through a set of French windows.

In the large spaces rugs have been used to define different areas – the sofas sit on a striped, cream-coloured rug, leaving space around the outside for circulation. A similar idea has been used to define the dining area, the library, and the sleeping space.

↓ The hard-edged lines of the walnut and glass bathroom are offset by the round shape of the limestone bath.

→ The luxurious bathroom features a stunning sauna set in a walnut and glass case, and a bowl-shaped limestone bath designed by Claudio Silvestrin for the Italian manufacturer Boffi. Limestone is also used in the flooring.

↑ The large open living room in the house
of Swedish glass, ceramic, and textile designer
Lena Bergström includes examples of her
colourful fabrics in the sofa and floor cushions.
The sliding linen blinds are also her design.

modernist apartment – stockholm, sweden

Purity, colour, and light are key to the work of glass, ceramic, and textile designer Lena Bergström. The themes are also to be found in her Stockholm apartment, which she shares with her husband Olle Johansson. Their home is in a Modernist post-war block close to Stockholm's city centre; at street level there is a flower shop and café, while Bergström's apartment is on the top level, with fantastic city views. The apartment itself has an unusual layout – the entrance opens into the long kitchen and dining area, which has a small outside balcony, stairs then lead down to a large open-plan living room, studio, bedrooms, and bathroom. It is painted white throughout and filled with plenty of natural sunlight.

The upper kitchen and dining area has a long, galley kitchen with white fitted units; the white dining table is surrounded by Arne Jacobsen Series 7 chairs. On window ledges and along the centre of the table is a selection of Bergström's glass work for the well-known manufacturer Orrefors. Downstairs, the main living room contains more glass and ceramic designs, as well as unusual window blinds designed by Bergström. They are made of large panels of translucent linen that slide across the windows and diffuse the light. The plump floor cushions in bright primary colours are from her collection for Designer's Eye. An intriguing feature of the living room is the original, raised corner fireplace. The main part of the L-shaped living area has two dark grey sofas, from B&B Italia, a coffee table, and floor cushions; the adjoining, smaller area is an office. Because Bergström and Johansson both work from home they like to keep the place as uncluttered as possible, so, throughout the apartment, furnishing and decoration has been kept to a minimum.

design directory

Designers, manufacturers, and retailers

Artek
Eteläesplanadi 18
00130 Helsinki, Finland
☎ 00358 9 6132 5277
@ www.artek.fi
Established to make Alvar Aalto furniture, but now incorporating contemporary designs; also in the UK:

Artek UK Sales
13 New North Street
London WC1N 3PJ
☎ 0044 20 7420 5913
and in the USA:

Herman Miller Inc
855 East Main Avenue
PO Box 302 Zeeland
MI 49464-0302
☎ 001 800 646 4400

Asplund
Sibyllegatan 31
11442 Stockholm, Sweden
☎ 0046 8 662 52 84
Nordic furniture and rugs by designers such as Jonas Bohlin and Thomas Sandell

Bo Concept
Club 8 Company A/S
Mørupvej 16
DK-7400 Herning, Denmark
☎ 0045 70 13 13 66
@ www.boconcept.com

← Sommerfugle, or Butterfly, chair by Nanna Ditzel, 1990, and manufactured by Fredericia.

Affordable contemporary furniture; stores worldwide including, in the UK:

Bo Concept
158 Tottenham Court Road
London W1T 7NH
☎ 0044 20 7388 2447
and in the USA:

Bo Concept@Paramus Inc
Harrows Shopping Plaza
141 Route 17 South
Paramus, NJ 07652
☎ 001 201 967 5300

Rupert Cavendish Antiques
610 King's Road
London SW6 2DX
☎ 0044 20 7 731 7041
@ www.rupertcavendish.co.uk
18th–20th-century furniture & furnishings

David Design
Stortorget 25
SE-211 34 Malmö, Sweden
☎ 0046 40 30 00 00
@ www.david.se
Contemporary furniture and homewares

Nanna Ditzel
Klareboderne 4
1115 Copenhagen, Denmark
☎ 0045 33 93 94 80
@ www.nanna-ditzel-design.dk
Award-winning designer of furniture, textiles, and jewellery; furniture available in Denmark from Fredericia (see p183 for details)

→ Model no. 600 AJ stainless steel cutlery by Arne Jacobsen, 1957, manufactured by Georg Jensen.

Filippa & Co
51 Kinnerton Street
London SW1X 8ED
☎ 0044 20 7245 9160
@ www.filippaandco.com
Late 18th–early 20th-century designs; store run by interior designer Filippa Naess

Fiskars
PO Box 235
FIN-00101 Helsinki, Finland
☎ 00358 9 618 861
@ www.fiskars.fi
The world's most stylish scissors, plus garden tools, kitchen knives, and more; stores worldwide; in the UK:

Fiskars UK Ltd
Brackla Industrial Estate
Bridgend, Mid-Glamorgan CF31 3XJ
☎ 0044 1656 655 595
@ www.fiskars.com
and in the USA:

Fiskars Brands Inc
2537 Daniels Street
Madison, WI 53718
☎ 001 608 259 1649
@ www.fiskars.com

and in Canada:

Fiskars Canada Inc
275 Renfrew Drive, Suite 208
Markham, ON L3R 0C8
☎ 001 905 940 8460

Formverk Oy
Annankatu 5
00120 Helsinki, Finland
☎ 00358 9 6214 611
One of Helsinki's best interior design shops, run by Kenneth and Niklas Wikstrom

Fredericia
Treldevej 183
7000 Fredericia, Denmark
☎ 0045 75 92 33 44
@ www.fredericia.com
Contemporary furniture manufacturer, including classics by Nanna Ditzel; also in the UK:

SCP Limited
135–139 Curtain Road
London EC2A 3BX
☎ 0044 20 7739 1869
@ www.scp.co.uk

Gärsnäs AB
PO Box 26
SE-27203 Garsnas, Sweden
☎ 0046 414 530 00
@ www.garsnas.se
Contemporary lighting and furniture

Gustavsberg
PO Box 440
SE-134 29 Gustavsberg, Sweden
☎ 0046 8 570 391 00
@ www.gustavsberg.com
Amazing bathroom wares

Fritz Hansen
Allerødvej 8
3450 Allerød Copenhagen, Denmark
☎ 0045 48 17 23 00
@ www.fritzhansen.dk
Contemporary furniture including Arne Jacobsen; stores worldwide; in the UK:

Fritz Hansen
20–22 Rosebery Avenue
Clerkenwell, London EC1R 4SX
☎ 0044 20 7837 2030
@ www.fritzhansen.com

and in the USA:

ABC Carpet & Home
888 Broadway
New York, NY 10003
☎ 001 212 473 3000
@ www.abchome.com
and in Canada:

Void Interior Furnishings
334 Kings Street East
Toronto, ON M5A 3Y7
☎ 001 416 868 6600
@ www.voidint.com

The Home
Salt Mills
Victoria Road, Saltaire
Shipley, Bradford BD18 3LB
☎ 0044 1274 530770
Scandinavian designs for the home

Iittala
Hämeentie 135
FI-00561 Helsinki, Finland
☎ 00358 204 39 10
@ www.iittala.fi
Cookware & glassware, also Arabia ceramics & tableware, and Rorstrand porcelain; stores worldwide; in the UK:

Aria
295 Upper Street
Islington, London N1 2TU
☎ 0044 20 7704 1999
and in the USA:

OK
8303 West 3rd Street
Los Angeles, CA 90048
☎ 001 323 653 3501
and in Canada:

Scandinavian Arts Ltd
648 Hornby Street
Vancouver, BC V6C 3E8
☎ 001 604 688 4744

Ikea Svenska Försäljnings AB
PO Box 200
26035 Ödåkraväla, Sweden
☎ 0046 0476 81000
@ www.ikea.se
Founded 1943; Kungens kurva first & largest from 1965; branches worldwide;

↑ Flight Deck SL table with stainless-steel legs and concrete or wood-veneer top, Voss Co 1996.

in the UK:

Ikea
☎ 0845 355 1141
@ www.ikea.co.uk
and in the USA:

Ikea
@ www.ikea-usa.com
and in Canada:

Ikea
@ www.ikea.ca

Inhouse
28 Howe Street
Edinburgh EH3 6TG
☎ 0044 131 225 2888
Scandinavian tableware and accessories

Georg Jensen
Amagertorv 4
Copenhagen, Denmark
☎ 0045 33 11 40 80
@ www.georgjensen.com
Cutting-edge cutlery & silverware, plus Royal Copenhagen china; stores worldwide; in the UK:

Georg Jensen
14 Sloane Street
London SW1 9NR
☎ 0044 20 7235 0331

↑ Highly experimental chair exploring how a person sits, by Norwegian designer Peter Opsvik.

and in the USA:

Georg Jensen
683 Madison Avenue
New York, NY 10021
☎ 001 212 759 6457
and in Canada:

TORP Inc
345 Wellesley Street East
Toronto, ON
☎ 001 416 968 2768

Kinnasand
Lyddevägen 17
PO Box 256
SE-511 Kinna, Sweden
☎ 0046 320 303 00/40
@ www.kinnasand.com
Textiles, upholstery, carpets

Kompan
Korsvangen 11
5750 Ringe, Denmark
☎ 0045 63621250
@ www.kompan.com
Fantastic outdoor toys and playground equipment; stores worldwide; in the UK:

Kompan Ltd
20 Denbigh Hall
Bletchley, Milton Keynes MK3 7QT
☎ 0044 1908 642466
and in the USA:

Ardean Praino
6856 Eastern Avenue NW, Suite 210
Washington, DC 20012
☎ 001 800 735 9144
and in Canada:

Kimberly Crocker
6-376 Tillbury Avenue
Ottawa, ON K2A 0Y2
☎ 001 613 761 6210

Kvadrat
Lundbergsvej 10
DK-8400 Ebeltoft, Denmark
☎ 0045 89 53 18 66
@ www.kvadrat.dk
Elegant textiles; also in the UK:

Kvadrat
62 Princedale Road
London W11 4NL
☎ 0044 20 7229 9969

Luxo
Enebakkveien 117
PO Box 60 Manglerud
0612 Oslo, Norway
☎ 0047 22574000
@ www.luxo.com
Manufacturer of great lighting including the classic Luxo desk lamp; also in the UK:

Luxo UK Ltd
4 Barmeston Road
Catford, London SE6 3BN
☎ 0044 20 8698 7238
@ www.luxo.co.uk
and in the USA:

Luxo Corporation
36 Midland Avenue
Port Chester, NY 10573
☎ 001 800 222 5896
@ www.luxous.com
and in Canada:

Luxo Canada
1957 Le Chatelier
Lavel, Quebec H7L 5B3
☎ 001 450 688 5896
@ www.luxo.ca

Marimekko
Puusepänkatu 4
00880 Helsinki, Finland
☎ 00358 9 75 871
@ www.marimekko.fi
Clothes, accessories, and homeware; also in the UK:

Marimekko
16–17 St Christopher's Place
London W1U 1NZ
☎ 0044 20 7486 6454
@ www.marimekko.co.uk
and in the USA:

Mix
309 Sutter Street
San Francisco, CA 94108
☎ 001 415392 1742
and in Canada:

The Finnish Place
5463 Yonge Street
Toronto
ON M2N 5S1
☎ 001 416 222 7575
@ www.finnishplace.com

Montana Mobile
Bredgade 24
1260 Copenhagen, Denmark
☎ 0045 33 12 06 90
@ www.montanamobile.dk
Modular storage systems; also in the UK:

Aram Designs
3 Kean Street
London WC2B 4AT
☎ 0044 20 7240 3933

Nordic Interiors
130 Wigmore Street
London W1U 3SB
☎ 0044 20 7486 0330
@ www.nordicinteriors.com
Contemporary furniture and furnishings

Nordic Style
109 Lots Road
London SW10 0RN
☎ 0044 20 7351 1755
@ www.nordicstyle.com
Showcase of Swedish style

Northern Light
13 Stratford Road
Kensington, London W8 6RF
☎ 0044 20 7361 1500
Antique and modern interiors

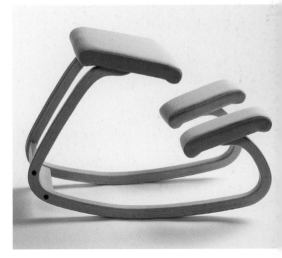

↑ Balans Variable kneel-on stool, 1979, designed by Peter Opsvik for Stokke.

Norway Says

Torbjorn Anderssen Design
Thorvald Meyersgate 15
N-0555 Oslo, Norway
☎ 0047 22 38 25 75
@ www.norwaysays.com
Furniture design company

Peter Opsvik

Pilestredet 27h
0164 Oslo, Norway
☎ 0047 22 36 56 56
@ www.opsvik.no
*Innovative furniture designer;
also in the USA:*

Hag Inc
108 Landmark Drive
Greensboro, NC 27409
☎ 001 336 668 9544

Orrefors

380 40 Orrefors
Sweden
☎ 0046 481 340 00
@ www.orrefors.se
*Sublime glassware;
also in the UK:*

Vessel
114 Kensington Park Road
London W11 2PW
☎ 0044 20 7727 8001
and in Canada:

Hemsley's
660 St Catherine Street
Montreal
PQ H3B 1B8
☎ 001 514 866 3709

← Theselius Rex chair by Mats Theselius, 1994, and manufactured by Källemo.

Piiroinen

Pohjoisesplanadi 21
00100 Helsinki, Finland
☎ 00358 9 667 632
@ www.piiroinen.com
*Smart furniture manufacturer;
also in the UK:*

Coexistence Limited
288 Upper Street
London N1 2TZ
☎ 0044 20 7354 8817
@ www.coexistence.co.uk
and

Tangram
33–37 Jeffrey Street
Edinburgh EH1 1DH
☎ 0044 131 556 6551
@ www.tangramfurnishers.co.uk
and in Canada:

Plan B Office Inc
91 Parliament Street
Toronto, ON M5A 3Y7
☎ 001 416 941 1010
@ www.planboffice.com

Louis Poulsen

Nyhavn 11, PO Box 7
DK-1001 Copenhagen, Denmark
☎ 0045 33 14 14 14
@ www.louis-poulsen.dk
*Legendary lighting manufacturer;
also in the UK:*

Louis Poulsen UK Ltd
Surrey Business Park
Weston Road
Epsom, Surrey KT17 1JG
☎ 0044 1372 848 800
@ www.louis-poulsen.co.uk
and in the USA:

Louis Poulsen Lighting Inc
3260 Meridian Parkway
Fort Lauderdale, FL 33331
☎ 001 954 349 2525

→ Atollo System shelving in oak-veneer plywood, by designer Andreas Engevik of Norway Says.

Røros Tweed

Tollef Bredalsvei 8
Norway
Great textiles

Rosendahl

Maglebjergvej 4
2800 Lyngby, Denmark
☎ 0045 45 88 66 33
@ www.rosendahl.com
Glass and tableware; also in the UK:

Aspects International
Brunswick Court, Victoria Street
Wetherby, West Yorkshire LS22 6RE
☎ 0044 1937 582626
@ www.aspectsinternational.com
and in the USA:

Karikter
19 Prince Street
New York, NY 10012
☎ 001 212 274 1966
@ www.karikter.com
and in Canada:

Urban Mode
389 Queen Street West
Toronto, ON M5V 2A5
☎ 001 416 591 8834
@ www.urbanmode.com

Royal Copenhagen

Amagertorv 6
DK-1160 Copenhagen, Denmark
☎ 0045 33 13 71 81
@ www.royalcopenhagen.com

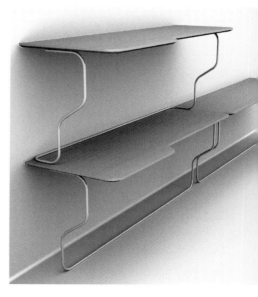

↑ Biri sideboard in lacquered MDF with steel legs,
by Espen Voll of design company Norway Says.

Classic porcelain and houseware;
also in the UK at department stores and:

Georg Jensen
14 Sloane Street
London SW1 9NR
☎ 0044 20 7235 0331

SCP Limited
135–139 Curtain Road
London EC2A 3BX
☎ 0044 20 7739 1869
@ www.scp.co.uk
Huge furniture showroom with
lots of Scandinavian design names

Skandium
72 Wigmore Street
London W1H 9DL
☎ 0044 20 7935 2077
@ www.skandium.com
Emporium of Scandinavian modern design
and also at:

Selfridges
400 Oxford Street
London W1A 1AB
☎ 08708 377377
and

Selfridges
1 The Dome, The Trafford Centre
Manchester M17 8DA
☎ 08708 377377

Stelton
Gammel Vartov Vej 1
DK 2900 Hellerup, Denmark
☎ 0045 39 62 30 55
@ www.stelton.com
Manufacturer of houseware including
the famous Arne Jacobsen stainless-steel
coffee set; also in the UK:

Vessel
114 Kensington Park Road
London W11 2PW
☎ 0044 20 7727 8001
and in the USA:

Bliss Home
121 Newbury Street
Boston, MA 02116
☎ 001 617 421 5544
@ www.blisshome.com
and in Canada:

Kilian International Design
1110 Kensington Road NW
Calgary, AB T2N 3P1
☎ 001 403 270 8800
@ www.kilian.ca

Stokke
N-6260 Skodje
Norway
☎ 0047 70 24 49 00
@ www.stokke.com
Ergonomic furniture manufacturer,
famous for the Håhjem kneel-on chair;
also in the UK:

Stokke UK Ltd
3 The Old Stables

Shredding Green Farm
Langley Park Road, Iver
Buckinghamshire SL0 9QS
☎ 0044 1753 655873
and in the USA:

Ars Vivendi
161 Homer Avenue
Palo Alto, CA 94301
☎ 001 877 528 3727
@ www.arsvivendi-usa.com

Svedbergs of Sweden
717 Fulham Road
London SW6 5UL
☎ 0044 20 7371 9214
@ www.svedbergs.co.uk
Amazing bathrooms

Svenskt Tenn
Strandvägen 5
PO Box 5478
SE-11484 Stockholm
Sweden
☎ 0046 8 670 16 00
@ www.svenskttenn.se
Furniture and home furnishings,
including designs by Josef Frank

Mats Theselius
Adesbersvagen 4
SE-27332 Tomelilla
Sweden
☎ 0046 4 171 52 08
@ www.theselius.com
Contemporary furniture designer

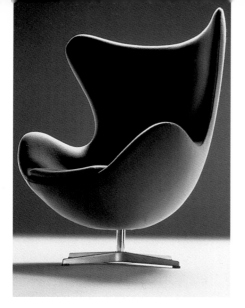

↑ Model no. 3316 Egg chair by Arne Jacobsen, 1958, and manufactured by Fritz Hansen.

Twentytwentyone

Twentytwentyone showroom
18C River Street, London EC1R 1XN

☎ 0044 20 7837 1900
@ www.twentytwentyone.com
Secondhand design classics; agents for Snowcrash designers and makers

Unique Environments

33 Florence Street
London N1 2FW

☎ 0044 20 7226 3006
@ www.uniquenvironments.co.uk
Home-style & tableware by Stelton & Iittala

Vessel

114 Kensington Park Road
London W11 2PW

☎ 0044 20 7727 8001
Glass and ceramics including works by Swedish designer Lena Bergstrom

Vipp

Sturlasgade 12 G
DK-2300 Copenhagen, Denmark

☎ 0045 45 88 88 00
@ www.vipp.dk
Possibly the world's most stylish waste bins; also in the UK at department stores and:

SCP

135–139 Curtain Road
London EC2A 3BX

☎ 020 7739 1869
@ www.scp.co.uk

and in the USA:

Waterworks

503 North Wells Street
Chicago, IL 60610

☎ 001 312 527 4668
@ www.waterworks.com
and in Canada:

Caban

2912 Granville Street
Vancouver, BC V6H 3J9

☎ 001 604 742 1522
@ www.clubmonaco.com

Vola

Lunavej 2
DK-8700 Horsens, Denmark

☎ 0045 70 23 55 00
@ www.vola.dk
Architectural ironmongery including classic taps by Arne Jacobsen

Voss Co

Carl Jacobsensvej 16, 13
DK 2500 Valby, Denmark

@ www.vco.dk
Contemporary furniture manufacturer

Wood Focus

PO Box 284 (Snellmaninkatu 13)
00171 Helsinki, Finland

☎ 00358 9 686 5450
@ www.woodfocus.fi
Database of Scandinavian wood industry

Wood.forgood

@ www.woodforgood.com
Database of Scandinavian woods and how they are used

Woodnotes

Tallberginkatu 1B
00180 Helsinki, Finland

☎ 00358 9 694 2200
@ www.woodnotes.fi
Textile manufacturer, including paper rugs; also in the UK:

Skandium

72 Wigmore Street
London W1U 2SG

☎ 0044 20 7935 2077

Architects

Claesson Koivisto Rune Arkitektontor

Sankt Paulsgatan 25
SE-118 48 Stockholm
Sweden

☎ 0046 8 644 58 63
@ www.scandinaviandesign.com/
claesson-koivisto-rune

Entasis (Signe + Christian Cold)

Sankt Peders Str 34a
1453 Copenhagen, Denmark

☎ 0045 3333 9525

Claes Von Hauswolff

BAS, Blekholmsterassen 50
111 64 Stockholm, Sweden

☎ 0046 8 24 40 00
@ www.basretail.com

Gunnar Tarras Hollström

Jakob Westinsgatan 6
112 20 Stockholm, Sweden

☎ 0046 8 651 03 23
@ tarras@swipnet.se

Claus Hermansen

Carl Jensens Vej 19
8260 Viby JM, Denmark

☎ 0045 87 34 07 55
@ www.claus-hermansen.dk

Carl-Viggo Hølmebakk

Sofiesgate 70
0168 Oslo, Norway

☎ 0047 22 46 76 00

Knud Holscher

Vermundsgade 40
2100 Copenhagen, Denmark

☎ 0045 3929 1001
@ www.knudholscher.dk

Jarmund/Vigsnæs A.S. Arkitekter

Hausmannsgate 6
0186 Oslo, Norway

☎ 0047 22 99 43 43
@ www.jva.no

Kjellander & Sjöberg Arkitektkontor

Triewaldsgränd 1

111 29 Stockholm, Sweden

☎ 0046 8 411 54 10

@ www.ksark.se

Birger Lambertz-Nilsen

Himarborg Torg

0179 Oslo, Norway

☎ 0047 22 99 44 50

Landström Arkitekter

Alsnögatan 12,

116 41 Stockholm, Sweden

☎ 0046 8 679 90 60

@ www.landstrom.se

Mette Lange

Strandgade 100, bygn N

1401 Copenhagen, Denmark

☎ 0045 55 99 98 19/70 20 19 21

@ www.mettelange.com

Søren Robert Lund Arkitekter

Store Kongensgade 110E, 1.sal

DK-1264 Copenhagen

Denmark

☎ 0045 3391 0100

@ www.srlarkitekter.dk

Nyréns Arkitektkontor

PO Box 4709

SE-116 92 Stockholm

Sweden

☎ 0046 8 698 43 00

@ www.nyrens.se

Maria Sahlström

Sweden

☎ 0046 8 4414 800

Sandell Sandberg

Riddargatan 17 D II

SE-114 57 Stockholm

Sweden

☎ 0046 8 506 217 00

@ www.sandellsandberg.se

Adser Schack

Granvej 2, Falsled

5642 Millinge

Denmark

☎ 0045 62 68 14 44

@ adser.schack@mail.dk

Anna von Schewen

Guldgränd 1

S-118 20 Stockholm

Sweden

☎ 0046 8 6436220

@ www.annavonschewen.com

Studio Suonto Oy

Oravannahkatori 1

02120 Espoo, Finland

☎ 00358 9 45 20 520

Jyrki Tasa

Kalevankatu 31

00100 Helsinki, Finland

☎ 00358 96 86 67 80

@ www.n-r-t.fi/Tasa

↓ Flight Deck coffee table with aluminium legs and concrete or wood-veneer top, Voss Co 1994.

index

acknowledgments

From the author:

First, I'd like to thank every architect and designer who has contributed to this book – without your inspiring work this project would have been impossible. I'd also like to thank the team at the Nordic Timber Council for their help, Liberon Waxes for information on wood treatments, the team at Artek for a fascinating tour round the works of Alvar Aalto, and the Danish Design Council for help in bringing to life the Arne Jacobsen story. In terms of production, thanks to editors Emily Anderson and Lara Maiklem, picture researcher Helen Stallion, and designer Geoff Borin for their boundless enthusiasm in making this a book we can all be proud of.

Picture credits:

Mitchell Beazley would like to acknowledge and thank the following for supplying photographs for inclusion in this book:

Alvar Aalto Museum 135; Maija Holma: 11, 22b, 23; Maija Vatanen: 79t

Arkitektens Forlag/K. Helmer-Petersen/Architect: Haldor Gunnlögsson 2–3; Jørgen Strüwing/Architect: Arne Jacobsen: 7, 10, 78

Arkitekturmuseet, Stockholm 17; Architect: Ralph Erskine: 130; Max Plunger/Architect: Leonie & Charles Geisendorf 128; Sune Sundahl/Architect: Stig Ancker 79b

Artek 138tl, 138tr

Bo Bedre/GV Press Front cover, 28, 29, 34bl and br, 35, 42, 43t and b, 44, 45, 46, 47, 52, 53, 54, 55bl and br, 100, 101, 102tl and tr, 103, 129, 144, 145, 146, 147t and b

Bridgeman Art Library/Mother's and Little Girls' Room Carl Larsson 8b

Camera Press 162, 163

Case Study/Gitte Staerbo 154, 155

Nanna Ditzel Design 182t

Solvi Dos Santos/Architect: Div.A 66–67

Patrik Engquist/Architect: Claesson Koivisto Rune 166 bl and br, 167, 168, 169, 170, 171

Peter Grant Back cover

Fritz Hansen 139bl and br

Lars Hallen/Design Press 4, 5, 72, 73, 116, 117, 118, 119, 120, 121t and b; Architect: Nanna Ditzel 81, 136

Carl-Viggo Hølmebakk 1, 26

Jesper Hom/Architect: Vilhelm Wohlert 27

House of Pictures ApS/Kim Ahm/Vivien Boje 150, 151, 152, 153; Kim Ahm/Jens Barslund 48t and b, 49; Kim Ahm/Inger Skaarup 97tl; Lise Jensen/ Kristian Krogh 36, 37tl and tr; Anders Norrsell /Skribent Bitte E:son Forsberg 40, 41; Helén Pe & Roth & Stone Productions 32, 33 bl and br, 82, 83, 84, 85, 148, 149tl and tr, 156, 157, 158, 159; Gert Skaerlund Andersen/Vivien Boje 96, 97tr

Arne Jacobsen 182b, 188

Jarmund Vigsnaes A.S. Arkitekter M.N.A.L/Nils Petter nispe@datho.no 14–15, 64, 65, 98 bl and br, 99, 104, 105

Anders Kavin/Gitte Staerbo 38, 39, 56, 57,

Nathalie Krag/Architect: Entasis 134, 140bl and br, 141, 142, 143

Carl Larsson-gården 18, 19, 20, 21

Library of the Royal Danish Academy of Fine Arts, Architectural Drawings Collection 74, 75

Ake E:son Lindman/ Architect: Claesson Koivisto Rune 176, 177t and b, 178, 179; Architect: Finn Juhl 131t and b, 132, 133; Architect: Landström Arkitekter AB 92, 93, 94, 95, 112, 113, 114, 115; Architect: Nyrens Arkitektkontor 164, 165; Architect: Maria Sahlstrand 124-125, 172, 173, 174, 175; Architect: Sandell Sandberg/Landström Arkitekter AB: 50, 51tl and tr; Architect: Anna von Schewen 108, 109, 110, 111; Architect: Gert Wingårdh 68 bl and br, 69

Louis Poulsen 139t

Marimekko 13

Museum of Finnish Architecture 16, 126, Simo Rista/Architect: Aarno Ruusuvuori 76t and b, 77

Norway Says 186b, 187

Norwegian Architecture Museum/Jiri Havran/Architect: Sverre Fehn 24, 25

Peter Opsvik 184, 185

Verner Panton Design 137

Michael Perlmutter/Architects: Kjellander & Sjöberg Arkitektkontor AB: 160–161

Thomas Petri/Gitte Staerbo 30, 31,

Max Plunger 8t, 127, Architect: Alvar Aalto 22t,

Sandell Sandberg 106t and b, 107

Søren Robert Lund Arkitekter MAA PAR: 58, 59

Stockholm Stadsmuseum/Britt Olstrup 9

Studio Nurmesniemi Ky 80

Jacob Termansen/Gitte Staerbo/Architect: Mette Lange 70–71, 86, 87, 88bl and br, 89, 90–91

Mats Theselius AB 186t

Chris Tubbs 12, 180, 181tl and tr

Voss Co 183, 189

Stefan Wagenbrenner/Architect: Jorn Utzon 6

Wood Focus/Comma Pictures/Mikka Auernitty/Architect: Sebastian Lonqvist 63; Esko Jämsä/Architect: Juha Paldanius 60; Jussi Tianen/Architect: Jyrki Tassa 61, 123; Esko Jämsä/Architect: Studio Suonto Oy 62

Wood.for good/Architect: Jyrki Tassa 122, 123

Key: t = top; b = bottom; l = left; r = right